MEMO GIDLEY'S

SECRETS OF SPEED

FOR SHIFTER KART RACING

Published by Secrets of Speed,
Oakville, Ontario, Canada L6L 5W2

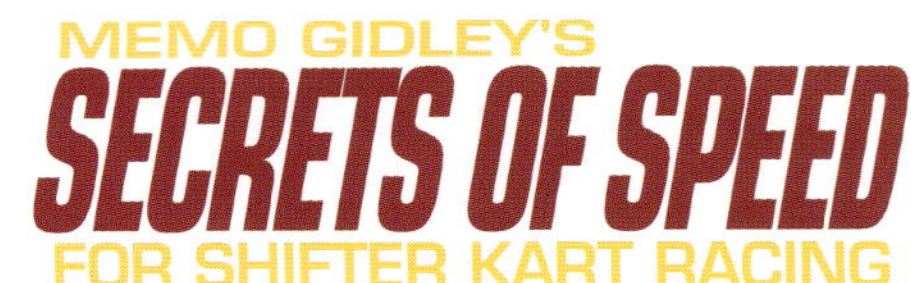

Author: Jeff Grist
Co-author: Memo Gidley
Design and Production: Craig Ketchen, Pillar Design
Cover Design and Layout: Jeremy Ortega, High Speed Productions
Website Design: Rachel Ponke, Area 50 Design
Photography: Jeff Deskins, Shiftsport Imagery
Copy Editor: Caroline Owen, Caroline Owen Services
Printing: Steve Trypis, ProPress Printers Inc.
Administration: Helen Grist

Area 50 Design Inc.
President: David Grant
Creative Director: Tiffany Strugnell
Production Manager: Sandra McDermott

TAP Internet Access Ltd.
Technical Support: Jon Simkins
Technical Support: Dave Wiese

Special thanks to Earl Ma for the rain shots and
Terry Neill of Nautilus of Marin for use of his health club.

First Printing February 2003
ISBN 0-9732595-0-7

Published by Secrets of Speed,
Oakville, Ontario, Canada L6L 5W2

Printed in Canada.

We welcome comments and suggestions regarding this book. Please write to us at:
Memo Gidley's Secrets of Speed
2125 South Service Road West
Oakville, Ontario, Canada L6L 5W2

www.mgsecretsofspeed.com

BEFORE YOU BEGIN

Statement of Liability

This book provides a general overview of what it takes in materials, labor and equipment to maintain a shifter kart. There is no guarantee that the operation of a shifter kart will comply with the codes governing your state, county, municipality, etc. The author, co-author and/or publisher take no responsibility for any injuries sustained in a kart maintained using this book. Always consult your owner's manual. No affirmation, promise or description relating to this book shall be deemed part of the basis of the party's bargain. The author, co-author and/or publisher does not know or have a reason to know of any particular purpose for which the buyer requires this book and does not represent that it shall be it for any particular purpose.

Notice of Disclaimer

Kart racing is a dangerous undertaking and no responsibility can be taken by any persons associated with this book, the author, co-author, the publisher, or any person or persons associated here where, for injury sustained as a result of or in spite offollowing the suggestions or procedures offered here in.

Every attempt has been made to present the information contained in this book in a true, accurate, complete and original form. The information contained in this book was prepared with the best information that could be obtained at the time of publication. All recommendations are made without any guarantee on the part of the authors or the publisher, and any information utilized by the reader is done so strictly at the readers risk. Because the use of information contained in this book is beyond the control of the authors or publisher, liability for use is expressly disclaimed.

Quick Safety Note

Always wear safety goggles when using power tools. Always read and observe all safety precautions provided by any tool or equipment manufacturer, and follow all accepted safety procedures. Always read the owner's manual carefully. Always remember to secure clothing and hair before operating any power tools. Always remember to keep all electrical cords and power tools away from water.

Above all, have common sense and be aware of your surroundings. Failure to follow important cautionary instructions may lead to circumstances, which might cause significant bodily injury or harm.

Important Warning

Your shifter kart can be dangerous; it should be treated with respect and maintained properly as outlined by the manufacturer. Always check for loose hardware, cracks and leaks before driving your kart. Make sure all components and wheels are secure at all times. Wear proper safety equipment when driving your kart. Drive your kart at approved and insured facilities only. Do not operate your kart in a reckless and unsafe manner.

Always drive safely.

Understanding the Big Picture

Introduction by Memo Gidley

Memo always has time for the kids.

I have raced in cars that most people only dream about. I have raced for teams that spend millions of dollars a year to try to be the best. I have driven for sponsors that are household names. I have been flown to car races on Lear jets. In my racing career, I have accomplished many great goals in the world of automobile racing. I remember my best race like it was yesterday. To achieve it, took years of preparation. That race without a doubt was the most satisfying race of my career. It was the 1999 Super Nationals held in Las Vegas, a race that I won. That race was not in a car, that race was in a shifter kart.

When I bought my first kart, I was so excited that I had to pull over a few times on the way home just so that I could look at it. I was a rookie in every sense of the word. I remember my first day driving. Driving that day, my first impression was how fast my new kart felt. I was so excited I didn't leave until dark. I never had any idea that karting would become such a huge passion of my life. I remember thinking I was going to do everything better. I had a lot to learn.

Memo's other favorite sport.

It was less than a few months after my first day at the track that a new friend, George Barros helped me to get into an opportunity of a lifetime. George introduced me to his karting sponsors, Fausto Vitello and Eric Swenson, two men who would end up to be the most influential and helpful people in my racing career. I remember Fausto looking at my kart for the first time and telling me it was the dirtiest kart he had ever seen, and then proceeding to tell me how to prepare it right. I remember Eric walking through the Trackmagic shop, always stopping to make sure that I had access to every thing that I needed. And of course George, always answering my many questions on kart set-up.

It was while I was struggling at the time to raise sponsorship to drive cars that the real beauty of karting became clear. Success in Kart racing was equal to the work you put into it. I loved working on my kart and I wanted to win.

In this book you will find many of the techniques that I learned from years of practice and trial and error at the kart track. I have never been a person that accepts the norm and many of the things I do may seem excessive. The only reason I do things a certain way is that I feel they make me faster on the track. My advice to you is to experiment yourself. Take the techniques I use and try to make them better. You too can achieve great things in karting. Whether trying to be the best driver ever or just trying to have some good weekend fun. Karting is an exciting and rewarding sport. As I always say, dream big and work hard! Good luck, I'll see you on the track.

Memo at the office.

I want to thank two people who have been an inspiration to me. They are the number one reason for me being able to realize my dreams, my mom and dad. Although my Dad has since passed, my mom continues to support me in every way. And to my girlfriend, I couldn't do the things I do without you.

Welcome to Shifter Kart Racing

Preface by Jeff Grist

Welcome to the world of shifter kart racing. Whether you are a young racer building toward a career in motorsports or a recreational driver looking for the thrill of speed and performance, you have come to the right place. This book has been designed to move you through the learning curve quickly and maximize the performance of you and your kart. Knowledge is the most powerful tool you can bring to the track.

With a liquid-cooled two-stroke engine, a six-speed gearbox and slick tires, the performance of a shifter kart is like nothing you have experienced before. For those with a karting background, or those with motorsports experience, we will draw comparisons to help make the transition to shifter karts smoother. Shifter karting is high horsepower, high performance racing at it's best.

Each chapter is design to provide an ever-increasing understanding of your kart and what it can do for you. The book anticipates what you will need to know next as you move along the learning curve. Special Tips and Tricks are included in each chapter to detail the little things that can be the difference between just finishing and winning. The book is filled with loads of charts, diagrams and outlines that can be removed, copied and used for kart set-ups, tracking changes and monitoring progress.

As a foundation we will exam how the kart is properly assembled and explain how the design of the chassis helps a kart perform. As part of this examination we will outline the special role the seat plays in maximizing your karts performance. Next we will step into the world of the two-stroke engines and provide a solid base from which you can keep your power plant in top working order.

Other areas we will exam include tire maintenance, gearing set-up and data acquisition. Special attention is given to establishing a baseline for each key area of your kart. A common theme through the book is being prepared using all the same principals the top kart driver's use including setups for dry and wet weather conditions. Finally the book will explore racing and driving techniques specific to a shifter kart.

I would like to thank my wife Helen and my son Garett for all of their love and support. I couldn't have put this book together without them. Also, I would like to thank my parents, Lorne and Marion, for giving me the confidence to try to new things.

Have fun and race safe!!

Jeff's passion shared by many.

Jeff gets ready to run at Mosport.

Jeff finishes a great run at Barrie.

TABLE OF CONTENTS

warning

These are designed to bring your attention to potential danger, the possibility of injury or highlight a serious matter. Each and every warning should be taken seriously. Always use common sense and good judgment.

hot tip

These are some of the things that Memo has learned over the years that will help you move through the learning curve quickly all the way to the head of the field.

cool trick

These are designed to highlight a unique way of doing things, a special procedure or a short cut that will make working on your kart more fun and enjoyable.

GETTING STARTED

Overview

Now that you've purchased your shifter kart, it's time to take that first run. This chapter provides a quick introduction to the things you need to do before laying down those first laps. We will provide a general orientation and touch on many aspects of the kart, all of which we cover in more detail in later chapters.

Whether you purchased your kart new from a dealer or used from a local driver, it's now your kart. It is your responsibility to make sure the kart is safe to drive. Don't rely on someone else; it's your butt in the seat. A shifter kart is a big investment, so take the time and make sure everything is safe and secure. This will be your first impression of your new shifter kart; so make it a good one!

It is very important that you become familiar with how your kart is put together, so you can isolate problems before they become major repairs. Before you strap on your gear, let's go through a quick, general check and base line set-up.

On your mark...

Your first on-track outing should be pure orientation. You need to get familiar with the kart, the speed, the braking and the shifting. Do not rush this process to get a quick lap time. Use this first run as the groundwork to create good habits.

Your chassis manufacturer can be a good source for information. Go to their website and get all the information you can on your make and model. Your local kart dealer should be able to supply other key information you need, like chassis set-up and seat-mounting data. Don't be afraid to ask questions. Also, you need to build a dialogue with your engine builder. He will be vital in helping you avoid costly mistakes.

A shifter kart is very much the sum of its parts. To make a kart reliable, many of the key components are bolted to the chassis. You need to check all of these contact points and make sure everything is tight and secure.

Start by putting your kart up on a stand. Don't try to work on the ground; as it is easy to miss something. Next, get to the hardware store and stock up on cleaners, fluids, zip ties, cotter pins and rags. You need to get your tools organized and be ready to go. Be prepared and you won't get sidelined with unnecessary problems or delays.

Chassis Set-up

The first major step is to go through a complete nut and bolt check. See the Nut & Bolt Checklist on page 1 in the Appendix. Make a few copies and put them on a clipboard. This will help as a reference guide each time you go through your pre-run checks.

Put a wrench on every nut and bolt, checking for solid contact on the washers. Replace worn, bent or stripped bolts immediately. Many bolts on a kart need to be cotter pinned, C-clipped or safety wired. Cotter-pinned bolts require a hole at the end for the cotter pin to fit through. Bolts that are wired require the end of one bolt to be wired to the end of another. Always safety wire in the direction that holds the bolt tight. Some European karts have bolts with the ends machined, to accommodate a C-clip.

Get your kart on a stand.

warning

A shifter kart is designed strictly for use on a designated closed course. It is illegal for this machine to be operated on any public street, road or highway.

Get your tools ready to go.

warning

Nylock nuts can fail with extreme heat and should never be used to directly secure pipes and brackets. In these cases use a lock washer, double nut or one-time nut.

Safety wiring a front brake caliper.

Starting at the front with the steering system, check all of the hardware such as the spindle bolts, inner and outer tie rod jam nuts and the bolts holding the steering column at the bottom and at the steering post. All of the steering system bolts need to be cotter pinned or C-clipped. All of these connections are safety items that are required to pass technical inspection in competition.

The next area that needs attention is the brake system. Make sure the pivot bolt on the break pedal is pinned, and the pedal is free to move without binding. The connecting rod has safety clips at each end. You can use a small zip tie around the safety clip for added security. It is recommended that you attach a piece of braided wire from the brake pedal to the rear brake master cylinder as a safety backup.

For safety, the bolts holding the master cylinders in place need to be safety wired or cotter pinned. The bolts that hold the brake calipers to the mounting brackets will also need to be wired together. Whenever you are wiring a bolt such as caliper bolts, for safety, it is critical that the wire is attached in a way so that it pulls in the direction that the bolt tightens. This will help to insure that the bolts do not become loose. It is recommended that you use stainless steel wire and proper wire pliers. It takes a little practice to wire correctly, so be patient.

Look over the brake lines and make sure they flow smoothly and are secured with the proper clips or tye wrap to the frame. The goal is to hold the lines firmly in place without pinching them. With 125's, move the steering wheel back and forth to make sure the lines move freely around the spindles. The brake pedal connecting rod and the left tie rod should not interfere with each other when the steering wheel is turned from side to side. Check the brake fluid level and top it up if required. Be careful. If spilled, brake fluid will remove paint and tarnish most finished surfaces. We will touch on brake bias and brake bleeding in later chapters.

The next area to check is around the rear axle and bearing cassette-mounting supports, making sure the bolts are tight and secure. Check to make sure the axle is set to an even distance on both sides and set the hubs an equal distance from the end of the axle. Axle collars or setscrews used to hold the axle in the bearings should be checked for tightness.

Step back and make sure that everything looks right with the routing of fuel lines and coolant hoses. The flow needs to be natural and smooth, with no kinks or sharp turns. Leaking hoses caused by chaffing is a common problem with shifter karts. Keep an eye on sharp edges that could cut into a line. Remember that on a shifter kart everything moves and vibrates a lot.

The radiator needs to be firmly secured in place and should be mounted using rubber bushings to isolate vibration. Make sure the hose clamps are tight, and the end of the clamp is not hitting a fitting or bracket, giving the false impression that it is tight. Most karts run the cylinder head hose along the back of the seat and secure it in a way to keep chaffing to a minimum. When routing water lines, keep in mind that the top of the radiator should be the highest point of the cooling system. This is to ensure that any air in the system will get trapped in the top of the radiator and be safely released out the vent.

In either ICC-style or moto-style engines, the fuel pump should be mounted as close to the engine pulse fitting as possible. It can be

Proper inner tie rod end setup.

Checking the outer tie rod ends.

cool trick

Get a small oiling can and fill it with brake fluid. It is much easier and cleaner to fill the master cylinders with a few small squirts than pouring it out of the bottle. The oil can must be able to seal itself when not in use to keep the brake fluid from being contaminated by air and moisture.

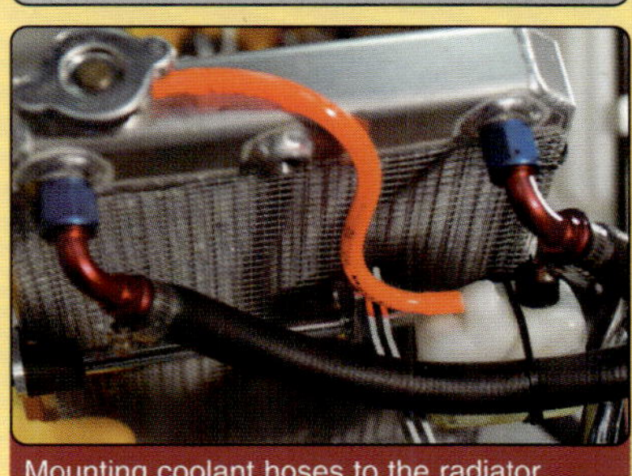
Mounting coolant hoses to the radiator.

Radiator mounting with rubber bushings.

Karts use a live axle setup.

Proper seat setup is important.

cool trick

When checking the seat, if any one bolt seems to angle differently from its mounting tab, use an adjustable wrench to bend the tab up or down. Remember, a little movement at the end of the wrench means a big change in angle on the tab.

hot tip

The number and tension of throttle return springs should be tailored for your driving preference. Too light a spring set makes the throttle application jerky, while too heavy a spring set makes the throttle application lazy.

bolted or zip tied into place. Make sure the fuel pump is secured in place and does not vibrate.

The final area to check is the front and rear bumpers, bodywork and floor pan. Most shifter karts run standard CIK side pods and nose cone. Nerf bars are one of the most critical safety elements and should be visually inspected for cracks or signs of wear. All of these components need to be secured using Nylock nuts. Look for connections that are isolated with rubber washers. Most of these connections need only be snug. A kart has both a front and rear bumper. For safety reasons, most karts are designed to have the front bumper bolts tight.

Seat Set-up

Most likely your kart has the seat already installed, or the dealer has installed it for you. If you need to install or move the seat go to Chapter 4 for details. Before you begin, you need to get the seat mounting specifications for your make and model of kart from the manufacturer.

The seat needs to be centered between the side seat posts. If there are excessive gaps on each side, remove the seat and bring the side supports closer together. Use hard plastic washers between the seat and metal supports to help prevent the seat from cracking when tightened. If the gap remains larger than a 1/2", pull the seat out and bring the side supports in closer together.

The back lip of the seat must always be forward of the axle, and the seat should be level across the top. If the seat looks a little left of center, that's normal and designed that way to compensate for the weight of the engine located on the right side of the kart.

Many karts come with extra seat struts. Seat struts are a way to tune the handling of your kart and will be discussed in further detail in Chapter Four. Check with your frame manufacturer to find the number of struts that are recommended for your height, weight and size as a baseline to start.

Engine Set-up

Now let's move to the engine side of the kart. As part of this chapter we will look at the throttle, carburetor, air filter, clutch, pipe and chain tension. In chapter five, we go into the engine preparation in more detail.

Start by checking the gas pedal, making sure the pivot bolt is cotter pinned and the pedal moves freely. It is recommended that the gas pedal have two springs. This ensures that the gas pedal will return even if one spring breaks. The throttle cable should flow smoothly up to the carburetor. If the cable has any kinks, replace it immediately. Make sure the outer casing does not touch the engine or pipe, causing the outer casing to melt. Use a cable casing that has a nylon inner housing, for smooth gas pedal operation.

Next move to the carburetor. The clamp on the carburetor should be snug and not cutting into the mounting boot. The intake boot is made of rubber, so be careful not to overtighten. Make sure you have the style of clamp that has rounded edges so it does not cut into the rubber boot. The fuel lines need to be tye wrapped to make sure no fuel leaks occur. Remove the air filter and check to see that the throttle slide closes completely. If it does not, loosen the throttle cable or pedal and adjust to the closed position. Tighten the cable, making sure the slide stays closed. Then to check for full throttle, push down on the gas pedal to make sure the slide rises all the way out of the carburetor bore. Adjust as necessary.

Put the air filter back on. The air filter or air box should be cradled with a mount. This will prevent the carburetor from moving or actually being jarred out of the intake manifold while going over bumps on the track.

Now we need to have a look at the ignition and coil. They should be at least four inches apart to avoid any interference from the electric impulses passing through the coil. Many times the ignition is mounted on the back of the seat. Try to keep both the ignition and coil clean and free of any grease or grime as these contaminants can make the plastic and rubber brittle over time.

The clutch cable should be free of bends and kinks. Again, make sure you use a cable casing that has a nylon inner housing to ensure smooth operation. When in place, the clutch cable should not bind or interfere with the movement of the steering wheel. It is important to check for endplay through the entire range of steering movement and not just with the wheel pointed straight ahead. You should have approximately 3/8" to 1/2" of play in the clutch lever. You should not require more than one inch of travel to engage the clutch. Any more than that and the outer plate could jump out of the basket.

Check the bump shift assembly and make sure everything is in place. Make sure the lever does not hit the steering wheel when shifting. When tightening the J-arm, make sure that it actually clamps down on the splines of the engine shaft. A loose connection will make shifting sloppy and can strip the spline, which would result in a very expensive repair. The J-arm should be mounted as close to vertical as possible, to ensure smooth, accurate shifts.

The final step is to set the chain tension. Loosen the engine adjustment bolt and loosen the engine mount bolts. This is a good time to check the bolts and the engine mount for cracks or wear. Push the engine forward until the chain has about 3/8" of play. Bring the engine adjustment bolt forward to touch the mount. Finger tight is good for now. Tighten the mount bolts, checking the tension as you go. With the engine mount bolts now firmly in place, tighten the adjustment bolt firmly against the mount. Make sure the chain guard is in place. This is a tech item and is good protection for you should the chain break. Also, the chain guard will keep your kart clean of flying grease.

Now that you have completed your routine check, you are almost ready to fire up your kart.

Getting it started

Before you fire up the engine, you need to add fluids to your kart. Make sure you follow all manufacturers recommended type fluids and specified amounts.

The transmission of a two stroke engine has a separate lubrication system from the crankcase. Most engine builders recommend 10w30 engine oil or ATF (Automatic Transmission Fluid). There are also specialized transmission gear oils from companies like Torco Oils that work well. Check with your engine manufacturer for the specification and amount of oil for your transmission.

hot tip

Keep in mind that moving the fuel pump and extending the pulse line increases the crankcase volume. This will have a negative effect on power output.

Always support your air filter.

The clutch should have some play.

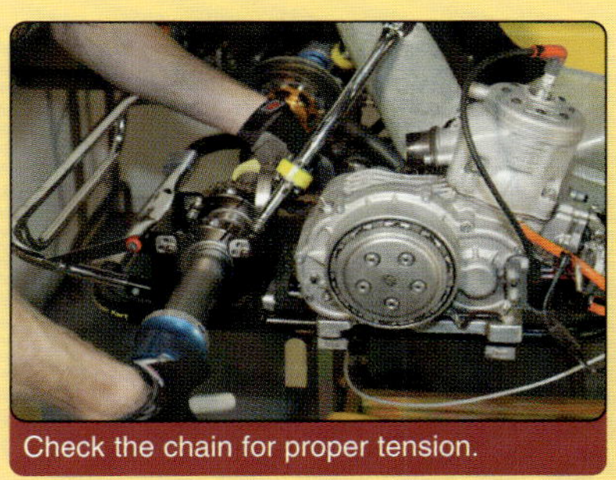
Check the chain for proper tension.

cool trick

To hold extra water solution for your radiator, use one of the plastic bottles that liquid laundry soap comes in. They hold the right amount of water and have a good pouring spout. Before you use it, make sure you rinse it out thoroughly.

Tipping the kart to burp out air.

hot tip

To keep from mixing up your fuel, it is important to always label your gas cans. Write on the can the important facts like mixed or unmixed, the type of fuel and/or oil, the mix ratio and the date of mixture. This will take out all of the guesswork.

warning

If you do not put the plug back in the cap and ground it to the engine, when you turn over the engine you will damage the electronics of the kart.

Next you need to look at the cooling system. Remove the radiator cap and fill the radiator with distilled water. It is recommended that you use distilled water in order to minimize corrosion. It is also a good idea to pre-mix a water treatment. This will not only increase the boiling point of the water, but will also lubricate the water pump. Once the water has been added, tip the kart on its right side. This will let any air in the system escape out the top of the radiator. Top up the radiator and replace the cap. Check for any leaks in the system and recheck the tightness of all the clamps.

Finally, you now need to mix some fuel for your kart. It is best to check with your engine manufacturer or engine builder to find out the correct fuel/oil mixture for your type of engine. A mixture of 20:1 to 25:1 is the range that most manufacturers recommend. 110-octane race gasoline is sufficient for most moto engines while ICC engines tend to use a 98-octane gasoline. This is a good, safe starting point that will err on the side of conservative. As you work with your engine builder and get familiar with the engine, you can fine-tune this gas/oil mixture for maximum performance.

You should use the darkest color gas can available, while still being able to see the level of the fuel through the outside of the can. The darker the can, the less likely the fuel and oil will deteriorate over time. For optimum engine and lubricating performance, it is recommended that any gas/oil mixture not be stored for longer than three weeks.

If the fuel delivery system is empty, you will need to prime the carburetor. Take the spark plug out and place it back into the cap. Place the spark plug against the cylinder head to give the spark a good ground. Next, put the engine in first gear and turn the rear wheel over. You should see the fuel begin to move from the tank into the fuel pump, and then into the carburetor. Stop the process and replace the plug when you see no more fuel going into the carburetor. Now you are ready to fire up your kart.

It is always a good idea to start your kart with a buddy. Have your friend stand at the front of the kart applying approximately an 1/8th of throttle. Put the kart in third gear and pull the choke lever up. Spin the rear wheels forward and be ready for the engine to fire. Once the engine starts, push the choke down and run the engine at a low RPM until the engine warms up.

After start up on a moto style engine use the bump shift lever to put the kart into neutral. For an ICC style engine with an external water pump driven off the axle, put the engine into first gear to keep the water circulating. With the engine fired, place your hand on the side of the cylinder, and feel for the engine to come up to temperature at about the same time as the radiator. If the temperature does not rise equally, the cooling system is not working properly. This is a sure sign of an air pocket in the cooling system. You will need to bleed the system as outlined earlier.

It is recommended that both water and cylinder head temperature sensors be installed on your kart. This is very important when you are driving on the track because it allows you to monitor the radiator and engine temperatures simultaneously. This will tell you if your cooling system is circulating the water properly.

Sufficient warm-up time is approximately five minutes or until the water temperature reaches 110° F or 43.3° C. When you reach optimum engine temperature, you can shut the engine off. If the idle is set properly, the engine should stall on its own when the throttle is released. If not, adjust the carburetor idle by adjusting the cable or backing off the idle screw. If your kart does not have a kill switch and does not stall on its own, put the engine in gear and apply the brake to stall the engine.

Base Line

To make sure the handling will be accurate and correct, you need to do a basic chassis set-up, before you go out onto the track. This will include setting the ride height, front and rear track width and tire pressures. It is recommended that you ask your kart manufacturer for a basic set-up starting point based on your height, weight and skill level. If this information is not readily available here are some quick generic settings to get you started.

Most karts have adjustable front and rear ride height. For the front, start with the middle setting in order to give you room for adjustment. If the rear of the kart has only two settings, high and low, choose the lower setting to begin with.

The front track width should also be set in the middle of the available range. For karts that use spacers, like 80's, split the spacers equally. For 125's that use a hub on the spindle, find the middle of the spindle and set the hub to that point. Rear track width should be approximately 54" for 80's and 54.5" for 125's. This is the measurement from the outside of the left rear tire to the outside of the right rear tire. Make sure the front hub bolts, and the rear hub bolts are tight.

Next you need to get a basic tire pressure. Each tire compound has a different optimum operating pressure. This information can be very difficult to find or not available at all. Generally speaking, the front tires should be 2 to 3 psi less than the rear tires. Normally, the harder the tire compound, the more pressure you will want to ensure maximum grip.

I would recommend 10 psi in the front and 13 psi in the rear for a soft compound tire, a 12/15 psi front/rear setting for medium compound tires and an 18/23 psi setting for a hard compound tires. These are COLD tire pressure recommendations. This means that your HOT tire pressures should be two to three psi higher after your run.

First Laps

Next is a quick snap shot of what you should do to shake down the kart and orient yourself. Be very aware of your surroundings. Keep an eye on the drivers around you as you come up to speed. Get comfortable and get a sense of what the kart is doing. We will go into each of these handling conditions in much greater detail in Chapter 10. For now, here are just a couple of tuning tips if your kart is way off.

If the kart does not want to turn, you have what is called understeer, or a push. This means the front end needs more grip. Make a quick change by widening the front track by moving the front wheels further apart. Move the front track out 1/4" (6 mm) at a time until this condition improves.

If the back of the kart wants to get sideways in the turn, you have what is called oversteer or a loose condition. This means the front end has too much grip and needs to be made narrower. Move the front track in 1/4" (6 mm) at a time until this condition improves.

If the kart is wandering as you go down the straight-aways, the

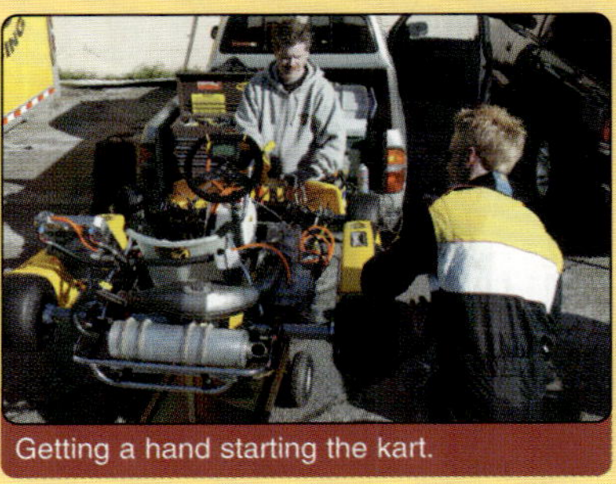

Getting a hand starting the kart.

cool trick

If you are at the track solo, you can use a small doctor's surgical clamp to hold the throttle an 1/8th open while you are spinning the rear wheels. You can usually clamp onto the cable somewhere near the throttle pedal. It takes a little practice, but once you master this, you will never need to rely on a second person to start your kart.

warning

You should never pull off the spark plug cap to stall the engine, as this will damage the engine electronics.

Driving position should be relaxed.

warning

Because a go-kart is not symmetrical, attempting to adjust the toe visually is a recipe for disaster and should not be attempted.

Check tire pressures HOT.

Put a clean rag in the plug hole.

warning

Dropping a spark plug on the ground can crack the inner porcelain, which could drop debris into the engine, leading to terminal engine damage. Never use a plug that has been dropped on the ground.

front may be out of alignment. It could have "toe out", where the wheels are pointing away from each other or "toe in", where the wheels are pointing toward each other. This is corrected by adjusting the tie rods. It is recommended that you put on the proper alignment gauges and check for the correct toe setting. This is usually between 1/16" to an 1/8" (2 mm) toe out. Check with your local kart shop for details on what alignment tools are available such as the Exact-Toe from RLV.

What to look for

When you come in from your first session, here is a list of some basic things you need to check. These basic checks should become habit for you after every on-track session. Have your charts ready so you can quickly write down the information.

The first thing to check is the tire pressure. It is CRITICAL to get the pressure readings immediately in order to get accurate HOT tire pressures. Compare these tire pressure readings to the COLD pressure settings when you went out. Each tire should have increased from two to three psi. Use the set-up chart on page 120 of the Appendix to track your tire pressure changes. Check the tires for any cuts or marks that may indicate a problem with the tire.

Next, check to see if you have any fuel leaks. Look for fuel under the seat and on the back of the kart. Try to isolate the cause by checking the lines for cuts, rubbing or chaffing. It is recommended that all fuel lines are secured with a small tye wrap to keep them from backing off their nipple.

Next, pull the spark plug and check for color. It should be a light brown, almost coffee color, in the middle porcelain area, and black on the outer metal ring around the porcelain. If the color is drastically different, consider a jetting change.

Next, slowly remove the radiator cap and check the water level. If the water level is down considerably, make sure the system is not leaking. Extreme caution should be taken when removing the radiator cap to avoid injury from hot water. Check the clamps and the hoses for leaks or cracks.

Finally, have a look at the chain tension. A new chain will stretch as it breaks in. If there is more than 3/8" (9.5 mm) of play, adjust the chain as outlined earlier in the chapter. As you move the engine forward, make sure that you are not pulling on any electrical, water or fuel lines.

Be sure to write down any notes as you run through the post-session review. This information will be very valuable as you begin to fine-tune your kart.

After you're done

After your first day at the track, you need to prep your kart for transport. This includes doing a good visual inspection. The main issue for transport and storage is dealing with the fuel in the system. Start by draining the fuel from the fuel tank. If you have a removable fuel tank you can take it off and dump the fuel into a gas can. You can also purchase a manual or electric siphon that will pull the fuel from the fuel tank.

In order to make sure the unused fuel in the carburetor does not run into the crankcase during transport, it is recommended that you remove your carburetor and drain the float bowl of all fuel. Removing the float bowl bolt on the bottom of the carburetor will do this. On some engines like the ICC-style engines, this can be done with the carburetor still attached to the manifold.

Basic Equipment

Here is a quick list of some basic equipment you need to keep your kart in top shape.

Tools

Start with good tools. Remember many shifter karts use metric hardware. Make sure you have metric T-handles, nut drivers, sockets and combination wrenches. Make sure your tools and equipment are in good shape. Worn or broken tools will only lead to problems with your kart.

Lubes and Oils

Your shifter will go through a lot of lubrication. Make sure you have chain lube, bearing lube, and spray-on lube. Check out Torco Oils at www.torcousa.com for a great selection of lubes and oils.

Cleaners

Keeping your kart clean is a must. It is always easier to work on a clean kart than a dirty one. Get your hands on some general-purpose cleaners for degreasing, along with lots of carb cleaner and brake cleaner. Check out Simple Green for a wide selection of cleaning products. Never use a water hose to spray your kart clean. The water will ruin the bearings on your kart.

Nut and Bolt Kit

Get your hands on a complete selection of nuts and bolts. Make sure you have all the sizes and cap styles for your kart. For a complete kit of those hard-to-find metric hardware pieces go to www.wewantmetric.com. They have a Pit Kit filled with most of the metric nuts, bolts and washers you need to keep your kart in shape.

Spare Parts

A kart has several items that are best described as consumables and should be replaced on a regular basis as part of an ongoing maintenance schedule. See page 109 in the Appendix for a Maintenance Chart. These are parts that wear quickly and should be replaced often. These include: fuel line, fuel filter, water hose, throttle return springs, throttle cable, wheel studs, wheel nuts, spark plugs and chain. It is recommended that you carry spares of all of the above listed items.

hot tip

You can create a siphon by taking the fuel line off the fuel pump and putting it in a fuel can. Remember to make sure your fuel can is lower than the fuel tank and clearly marked MIXED FUEL.

Find a setup that works for you.

Good chain lube is important.

Make sure you have lots of fasteners.

DRIVING TECHNIQUES

Be relaxed and comfortable.

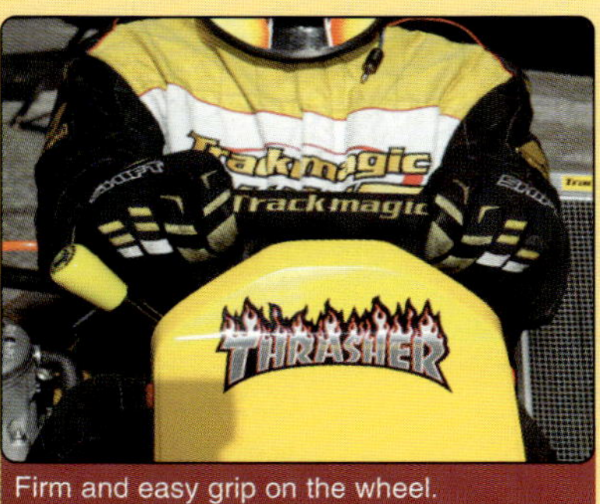

Firm and easy grip on the wheel.

Hands at 10 and 2 o'clock position.

Knees and elbows should be bent.

Overview

This chapter is intended to get you thinking about and understanding the driving line. You can't dial in your kart if you are not running the proper racing line. Having a complete understanding of driving line theory is an area most drivers overlook. Being quick comes from practice through trial and error.

Shifter karts have repeatedly proven to be the most versatile and effective tool for racers looking to improve their driving skills. In fact, most top race car drivers around the world attribute their success in cars to the lessons learned from karts. What makes shifter karts such an effective teaching tool is that they perform like an F1 or Champ Car, which are considered to be the fastest racing cars in the world. Yet, a shifter kart is much more forgiving if you get into trouble. Shifter karts are high performance racing machines that you can literally put into the back of your truck and take them to the track without a 30-person pit crew. In a shifter kart, smoothness and technique are rewarded with a fast lap time, while mistakes are amplified.

Driving fast on a racetrack is thought by many people to be something that you are born with; you either have it or you don't. While I agree that we are born with certain qualities like reaction times, quick decision-making and good eye sight, all of which can aid drivers in their ability to go fast, I also believe that understanding the basic driving techniques like those in this chapter are what makes certain drivers exceptional. Learning proper driving techniques are not just for the beginner or novice driver, it is the first step to being the most educated and fastest driver you can be.

Driving Position

In this section we will dissect the elements of how to find a comfortable position in your kart, which will help you to "feel" what your kart is doing. In a shifter kart the driver's movement and input have a major impact on the handling of the kart. We will look at hand position, body posture and line of vision.

Steering Input

A shifter kart will respond very quickly to steering input because of its short wheelbase and very wide track. Because of this, steering input needs to be very smooth and fluid regardless of the corner radius or speed. If the steering is too abrupt, the weight transfer is erratic and the tires can exceed their maximum traction causing the kart to slide. Many times this is diagnosed as a loose condition and you end up chasing a bad chassis set-up. The rate of turn in should be consistent and deliberate.

Hands

Hand position is something that is very personal to each driver, however there is some sound logic to where you place your hands. I recommend placing your hands in the ten and two o'clock position. This will give you the best leverage and control. With the amount of grip that current shifter karts generate and the abrupt power delivery, having good leverage is vital. It will allow you to not only experience less fatigue, but even more important, allow you to be aggressive with the wheel, if the handling is not ideal or the track has a lot of grip. You want to make sure that the steering wheel position is not too close or too far in front of you. I like to have a slight bend in my elbows with my hands on the steering wheel at the ten and two o'clock position.

Your hand position is vital to receiving input from the steering wheel providing you with much needed feedback from the kart. It is very important that you are relaxed in your shifter kart. Don't put a death grip on the steering wheel. This uses up energy and reduces your reaction times. Loosen your fingers as you drive down the straights. Not only does this help relieve arm pump for the occasional driver, but it also reminds even the more experienced drivers to drive loose, which will help them feel the racetrack better.

Body

Driving posture is an important part of learning to be smooth, fast and consistent. Of course a proper fitting seat, one that is snug, is the first step. Your back should be straight with the seat, making sure your shoulders are parallel with the ground.

A typical beginner mistake is to lean into or out of corners. Leaning into or out of corners affects the weight transfer and handling of your kart and makes it harder to be consistent. Keep an upright and strong posture in the seat, letting your arms work the steering wheel and your feet work the pedals. If you have to move your body to turn the wheel or push the pedals, you need to re-position the seat.

Also, try not to do the kart racer hunch. Because kart drivers are not belted in like racecar drivers, some tend to lean forward in the seat. Drivers that lean forward tend to have a lot of upper body movement, which changes the weight split of the kart and makes it hard to be consistent with their driving. The cure is to make sure you sit in the seat and let it support your back, hips and bottom.

Key Components

"Use the entire track," is a phrase you hear a lot in racing circles. In this section we will define the elements that make up a corner, including the entry point, the apex, the exit point, braking and accelerating, which will allow you to do just that: "use the entire track."

Turn In

The turn in is where the turn is initiated, where you begin to change direction and steer into the corner. It is critical to get this point right because this is the first step to a perfectly driven corner.

Apex

This is the tightest point, or clipping point, in any given turn. This is where you are the closest to the inner curbing. An apex is not always a point, but can be a stretch of track where you are the tightest to the inside of the turn.

Exit Point

This is the point where you have released, or straightened out the steering wheel completely. It is generally found just as you get to the outside edge of the track. This is important because how you come out of a turn determines how fast you will be going down the straightaway or how well you will be set up for the next turn.

hot tip

I have my steering block pre-drilled with multiple steering shaft positions. This allows me to always keep my steering wheel in a similar position when I change my seat position throughout the race weekend. If your steering block is not designed for multiple holes, I would recommend having different length blocks ready to be used.

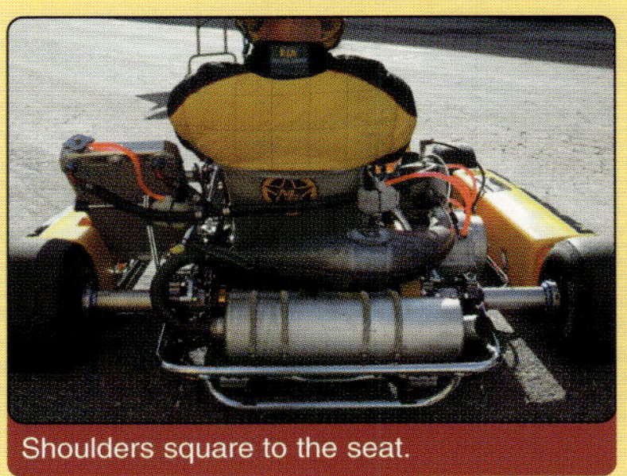

Shoulders square to the seat.

Feet in position ready to go.

Entering a corner.

Hitting the apex of the corner.

Exiting the corner.

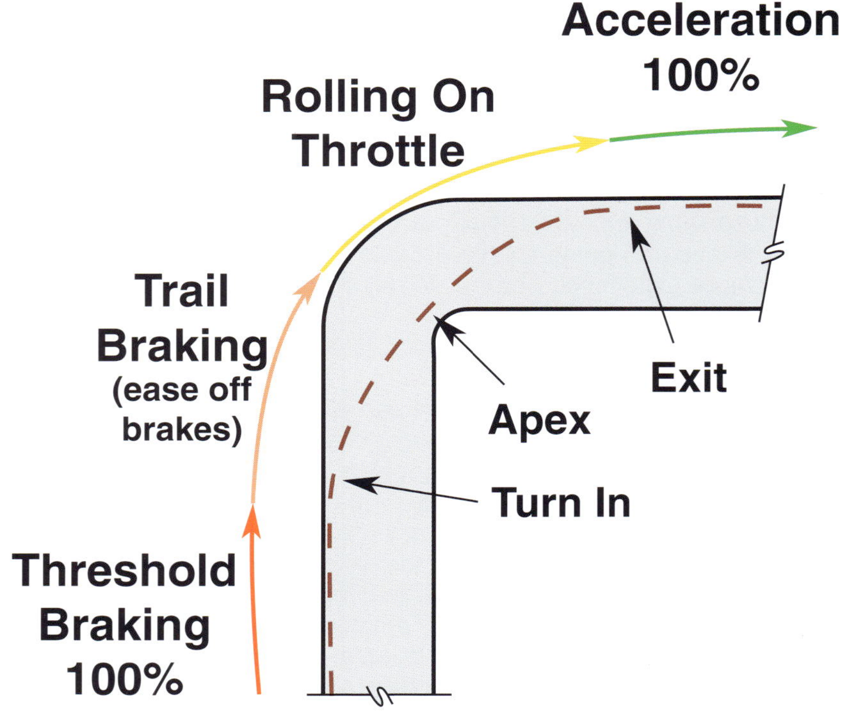

Braking

You will experience two types of braking situations heading into a corner: threshold braking and trail braking. If you are braking in a straight line, you are attempting to maximize the entire available grip for slowing down. Usually the maximum grip is achieved just before the tires lock up. In other words, you want to brake as hard as possible without locking up the tires. This is described as threshold braking, or braking at 100% of the karts limit.

As you turn into the corner, you need to transfer some of that grip for cornering or face going straight off the track with your tires locked up. This is where trail braking comes into play. Trail braking is the process of letting off the brakes as you enter into the corner so that you can use some of your available grip for cornering. The deeper you get into the corner, the more brakes you need to release to have grip for cornering.

Accelerating

As you complete the corner, you need to have some grip available for acceleration. As you unwind the wheel you increase your radius, which in turn provides more grip to be applied to accelerating. Just like easing off the brakes coming in, you need to squeeze on the throttle as you go out of the corner and onto the straightaway. Eventually, you will be going straight and require no grip for cornering. Once again you will be flat on the gas using 100% of the grip for acceleration.

This may seem a little confusing at first. Imagine that you only ever have 100% grip at any one time. It's all about a balance. Try to use that 100% grip consistently throughout the corner, whether it is under braking, turning, or accelerating.

The Racing Line

We know that racetracks are made up of a mix of corners and straightaways. Usually the most time spent on a racetrack is on a straightaway at full throttle. Because of this, your goal is not necessarily to have the fastest time through the corner, but rather the highest speed. That will allow you to brake as late as possible and allow you to enter onto the straightaway with a higher speed. This is important because you can travel more distance on a track at a higher speed, which means more time can be gained. A racetrack will consist of four general types of corners: 90-degree corners, entry speed corners, exit speed corners and combination corners.

The key to having fast corner speeds is to take the biggest radius possible through the corner. The basic formula is R = MPH, or the bigger the radius of the corner, the faster the mile per hour through the corner. It's simple when you think about it. This is the same reason why you can go through a sweeper with a larger radius faster than a hairpin with a tight radius. To get the biggest radius in any corner means starting all the way wide on the entry, going all the way tight at the apex, then going all the way wide again on the exit. In this section we look at each type of corner in detail and apply the various corner elements to demonstrate the perfect racing line.

Basic Corner

A basic or 90-degree corner can be thought of as symmetrical. The radius is fairly constant through the turn and the straightaway preceding the corner has about the same top speed as the straightaway following it. Based on what we know about the importance of straightaways, you would assume that both coming in fast (late braking) and exiting fast (acceleration) are equally important. Let's start with the braking. I always refer to braking late as slowing down less. Remember one way to slow down less is to have a higher corner speed. If your mid-corner speed is 35 MPH (56 KMP) and your buddy's is 30 MPH (48 KMP), you will need to slow down 5 MPH (8 KMP) less, which allows you to brake much later.

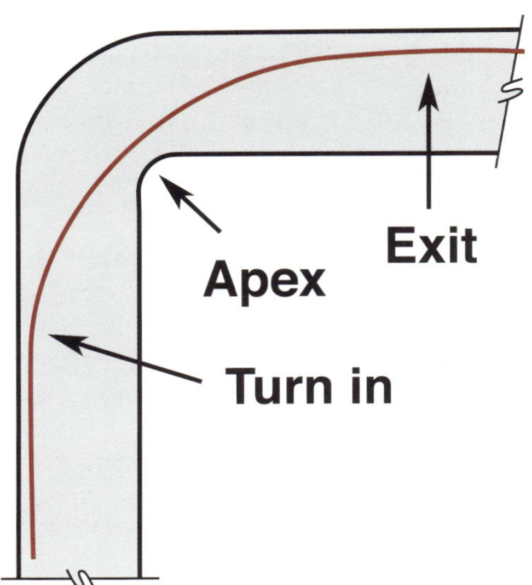

hot tip

Take the time to walk the track. Note slopes, off-camber sections, bumps, anything that might give you an edge. Always look for where you can find the most grip.

Making a smooth transition.

Jake Pierson hammers the exit.

Rolling out of the corner onto the straight.

Keeping things smooth and relaxed.

Remember, to have the highest corner speed, start by driving the largest radius possible. This means going outside on the entry to inside on the apex to outside on the exit. Apply maximum threshold braking on entry (just before lock up), ease off the brakes as you turn into the corner (trail braking), eventually applying no brakes, using 100% of the available grip in the middle of the corner. Then ease on to the throttle as you get to the exit of the corner, eventually reaching full throttle as you head down the straightaway.

Entry Speed Corner

Let's talk about my favorite, entry speed corners. An entry speed corner is positioned just after a fast straight and is followed by a short straight. For optimal performance on this type of corner, it is more beneficial to be on the gas longer at 80 MPH (128 KMP) as you enter the turn, rather than on the gas earlier at 30 MPH (48 KMP) as you exit the corner leading onto a very short straight. In other words, you can cover more racetrack at 80 MPH than at 30 MPH, which translates into a quicker lap time. Why is it my favorite? For me, it's the excitement of braking at the last possible second without flying off the track!

We can change our line, trail braking, and throttle application to make us faster on the entry. Start with the line through the corner. Again, our formula is R=mph, and remember that the bigger the radius the faster the mph. If we want to brake as late as possible, the goal would be to slow down less for the entry of the corner. We can do this by having a very large radius at the entry. The way we do this is to turn in early and to be as gradual as possible. The trade off is that by getting this bigger radius on the entry, the exit radius is much tighter.

Rolling through a transition.

Not a problem. Remember that entry speed is more important and is what we are after. Because we have the big radius on the entry, our braking point is much later, which means the entire process of trail braking continues much further around the corner than on our basic

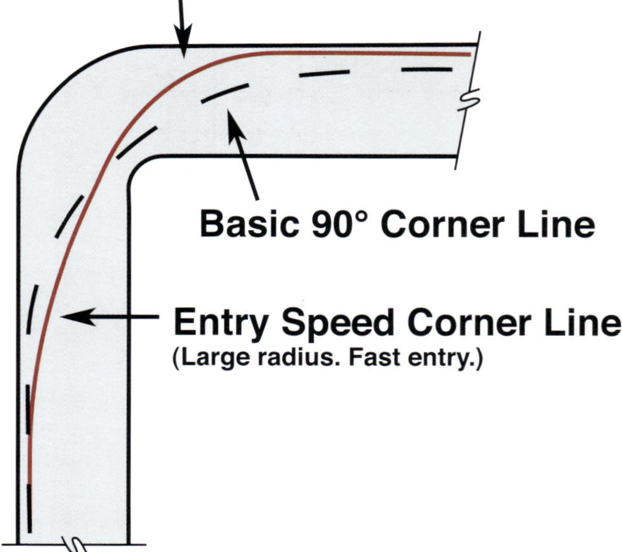

Use a pylon as a marker.

90-degree corner. Remember though, the same braking process still applies; ease off the brakes the tighter the radius gets.

As you can see, the apex is also further around the corner, and just like the later breaking point, we won't be able to roll onto the throttle until later. The technique of squeezing the throttle still applies to this type of corner just as it does in the basic 90-degree corner. Everything about driving is give and take. You can see that even though our technique may have lost us a tenth on exit, it gained back two tenths on entry for a total improvement of one tenth.

Remember that the brakes need to be applied properly. You want to squeeze the pedal, not stomp on it just because you are trying to brake very late. Applying brakes too aggressively does not give the kart enough time to transfer weight. Be quick with your braking, but be smooth and efficient.

Exit Speed Corner

The exact opposite of an entry speed corner is an exit speed corner. If you've understood the theory so far and can see the pattern developing, understanding the exit speed corner should be a snap. Like the name implies, it's all about exit speed to go fast. Unlike my favorite "braking as late as you dare corner," this one is all about braking early. This is because the straightaway entering is very slow but the straight following is very long and fast. If you had the choice of braking late at 40 MPH (74 KMP) or getting on the gas earlier for an 80 MPH (148 KMP) straightaway, what's it going to be? Of course getting on the gas earlier. Not as exciting as an entry speed corner, but equally important to making up time on the track.

Let's start with the turning radius. With our "the bigger the radius, the bigger the mile per hour" formula, we know that to get a fast exit we need a big exit radius. We also know that this is a compromise, and that by having a big exit radius, our entry radius is going to end up tight.

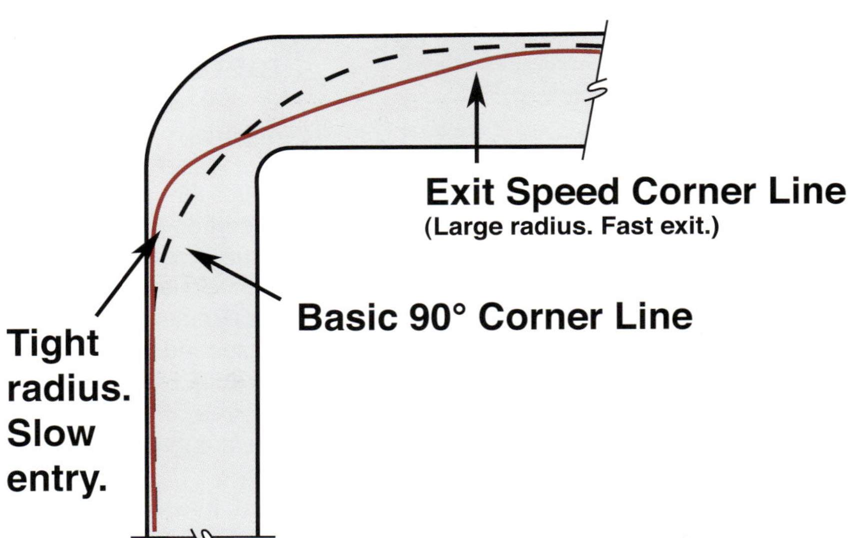

cool trick

Draw a map of the track, and identify which turns have priority in terms of lap times, and which have priority in terms of race strategy. Generally, the turn leading on to the longest straight is the most important for lap time and race strategy.

Using earplugs helps you hear the engine.

Be ready to shift on exit.

TJ Ross hits the gas.

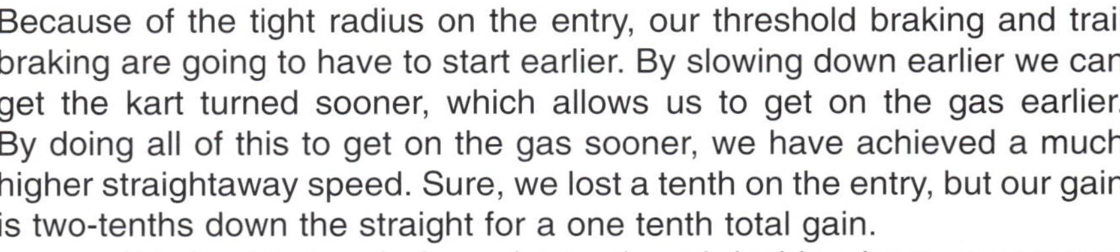

Because of the tight radius on the entry, our threshold braking and trail braking are going to have to start earlier. By slowing down earlier we can get the kart turned sooner, which allows us to get on the gas earlier. By doing all of this to get on the gas sooner, we have achieved a much higher straightaway speed. Sure, we lost a tenth on the entry, but our gain is two-tenths down the straight for a one tenth total gain.

It is best to break down the track and decide where you want to go faster. Basically, faster on the entry means slower on the exit, and slower on the entry means faster on the exit. It's pretty simple when you think about it.

Combination Corner

Combination corners or 'S' bends are also a compromise. If we draw the fastest line into the first turn and the fastest line into the second turn, you can see that the two don't connect. That means in order to stay on the track, we are going to have to sacrifice the line on one or both corners so that we can complete the turn. With what we now know about cornering, we must decide where we want to be fast.

Joe Janowski rolls past the apex.

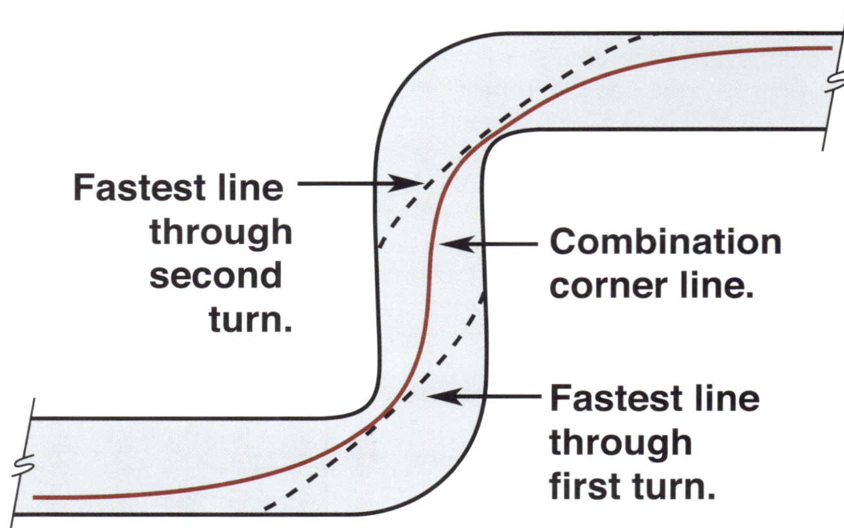

First, look at the straightaway heading into the combination corner and compare it to the straight leading off the corner. If the straight heading in is faster, then you know the entry has the most potential to gain time and that we want to slow down less, or brake as late as possible for the first part of the combination corner. Remember, in this situation we are willing to give up time in the second part of the combination, if we can gain time in the first part for a total net gain. If the straights were reversed, then the opposite would be true. If the straights are equal, then sacrificing a little on both parts of the combination turn is what you're after.

All the other techniques we already discussed, threshold braking, trail breaking and rolling onto the throttle to balance the kart at the very maximum grip level, still apply.

Completing an exit speed corner.

Kart Rotation

Once you start to master the proper line and driving technique, something called "rotation" will come into affect. Rotation happens when you have a combination of trail braking, maximum cornering speed, and throttle application. This technique allows the driver to get on the gas earlier, while staying on the track. When approaching the apex, the back of the kart slides slightly, allowing the kart to point down the road without as much steering input. Since the kart is pointed in a straighter line than usual, the driver can get on the gas earlier. It is important to roll slowly and as early as possible on to the throttle, to keep the slide going all the way to the edge of the track, maximizing the available grip and width of the track to attain maximum corner exit speed.

Looking into the entrance of a turn.

Driving Techniques

In this section we will look at some of the shifter kart driving techniques that will be used in laying down that perfect lap. Each technique is a unique discipline in itself and requires a great deal of practice. Start slowly and work your way through each of these key components. These techniques include using reference points, proper shifting and setting brake bias.

Matt Champagne looks ahead.

Reference Points

"Hit your marks." You hear this all the time in racing. It is important because hitting the defined marks means you are driving the kart exactly where you think it needs to go. A technique that helps with this is to get used to looking for landmarks such as a pylon, a line on the track, a hay bale, a grease spot, or anything else that is clearly visible and can be used as a reference point. It is important that you get into the habit of looking around, opening your field of vision. I actually look around both on and off the racetrack as much as possible when I drive. Keep your eyes moving constantly, looking down the track, always in the direction where you want to go.

The reference points will come naturally. Looking around will help you to be more consistent with your braking points, turn in points, apex/release points and acceleration points lap after lap. Of course it is always best to use reference points that cannot be moved, like a fence post or sign marker. Another great feature of reference points for new drivers is that they can act as indicators of how you are progressing. As you begin to become more proficient in your kart, you will find that your reference points may change. This is especially true for braking.

Kyle Martin sets up for a corner.

Some professional drivers view each section of a track as a page on a book. As you reach the exit point, you turn the page in your head and dig into the next section. This helps you to remain focused and "turn the page" on a bad section, making sure it does not affect the next section.

Shifting

Shifting your kart is a critical component to your overall lap times. Maximizing your speed is directly related to hitting your shift points as you

Matt Champagne holds his line.

Bump style shift lever.

are driving your racing line. Like braking and accelerating, shifting needs to be smooth and consistent. Many drivers are confused about the proper point to begin shifting up or down. Every track is a little different so there are no hard and fast rules. There are, however, some guidelines that I find work well for me.

When shifting up through the gears you need to lift off the throttle for a split second to free up the gearbox, allowing the gear selection change to happen smoothly. Currently no racing bodies allow electronic interruption to help with this like I use in a Champ Car. You want to just let off the throttle ever so slightly as you pull on the lever to shift up. I try to position my shift lever so that I simply open my hand, leaving my thumb still on the wheel, and pull the lever with my fingers. It takes a little practice and adjustment of the shift lever, but can make the shifting process a little cleaner and smoother.

The other big question is exactly when to shift. Most newcomers tend not to use the maximum power of the engine by either shifting early and "lugging" the engine, or shifting late and "over-revving" the engine. Some electronic dash displays come with shift lights that can be set for your engine. However the best way to learn the time to shift is through practice. This will only come with driving your kart and getting a feel for when the engine is in its "powerband."

Shifting up a gear.

The next big challenge is when to downshift. This is a little trickier and usually requires a bit more practice than upshifting. When downshifting, the idea is to select a lower gear at an RPM that won't lock up the rear tires. As you might imagine, if you are using 100% of the grip for braking, and then jam the transmission down one gear, rear tire lock up will be the result. The proper technique is to wait until the engine RPMs drop a little before selecting a lower gear. If you are downshifting more than one gear, try to space out your downshifts, again to allow the RPMs to drop a little in each gear before going down again.

The more advanced technique is to blip the throttle on your downshifts just before selecting the lower gear. It is really all about timing. The technique is to crack open the throttle for a split second while simultaneously pushing the shift lever into the next lower gear. If your timing is off, the transmission will not want to go down a gear. Too much of a blip will make the kart jump forward, while too little will cause the rear tires to lock.

The easiest way to think about this is when you blip on the gas you are attempting to match the RPMs of both sides of the transmission or both "gear stacks." The reason this is hard to do is because the neutral in between gears is very small. However, done successfully, blipping the throttle on the downshift will make for very smooth shifting.

Brake Bias

Getting ready to down shift.

Setting the brake bias on a 125cc shifter is very important. It is always amazing to me the number of drivers that rarely adjust their brake bias from track to track, let alone session to session. Improperly adjusted brake bias can easily cost you a tenth or two on a 30 second sprint track. Remember the front and rear brakes operate from different master cylinders. These master cylinders are connected at the top with a bias bar, which allows the driver to adjust the amount of rear and front brake that is applied as the brake pedal is pushed. A good setting to start with is a 55% rear and 45% front split.

The way to check this is to push down on the brake pedal with one hand while slowly turning the rear tire with the other hand. As soon as the rear tire becomes difficult to turn, I hold that pressure on the pedal and try to turn the front tire. A 55% rear and 45% front setting will have the rear tire locking up just before the front tire.

When doing this on the stand we have more rear brake. However, on the track we actually have a little more front bias. This is where the confusion comes in. Because most drivers realize that they want a little more front brake on the track, they assume the same is true on the stand. This leads most new drivers to mistakenly set their brake bias with way too much front brake. The reason is that they fail to understand that the rear brake has much less power and a lot more work to do than the front brake.

Let's think about why for a minute. In the front you have one brake caliper that stops one wheel. The rotating weight that it slows down, for example, is approximately six pounds. The rear brake on the other hand has to slow down two rear tires, a drive gear, a chain, a water pump gear and a metal axle that runs the width of the kart. The weight that the one rear brake has to stop is more than double the weight that a front brake has to manage. So, for this simple reason, setting a little more rear brake on the stand translates to the correct amount of front brake on the track.

Now, on the track there are characteristics that will tell you if your bias is set correctly. If you have too much rear bias, the rear tires will want to lock and the back end will want to go sideways. If you have too much front bias, the kart will want to dart on initial threshold braking, and turn in. Another sign of too much front bias is as you trail off the brakes and turn into the corner the front will pick up a hop.

Different tracks and conditions will also require a different setting. A track with a lot of sweeping corners requires much less front brake than a track with a lot of straight line braking zones heading into slow corners. The reason is that in straight line braking you have much more weight transfer to the front end, which means you need more power or bias on those front brakes. On light braking and sweeping corners, the opposite is true. I realize that adjusting your bias on the track without slowing down is difficult, but it is definitely something you want to learn to do. During a long race there are many things such as tire wear, fuel weight, and track conditions that will require a different bias adjustment.

Brake bias adjustment knob.

Brake bias set-up.

Setting the brake bias.

Adjusting the brake bias.

CHASSIS SET-UP

Putting it all together.

Shifter Kart 101

The basic design of any kart chassis uses a solid or "live" axle as it is sometimes called, which locks the rear wheels together by way of a single axle. By contrast, a racecar uses a differential in the rear end to help it turn through a corner, allowing the inside wheel to rotate less than the outside wheel as they travel through a different radius. A kart relies on weight jacking and the flex of the chassis, allowing the inside rear wheel to lift off the ground. This mechanical transfer of weight makes the solid axle act like a differential, helping the kart turn through a corner.

The simplicity of a kart's design is based on an unsprung chassis that will react in a predictable manner when forces are applied. Although a kart has no suspension, the entire kart does have many "sprung" characteristics. Like a racecar, much of this happens through the tires and is translated back to the chassis through the rear axle and front spindles. Wheel hop is an example of one of the affects that can occur as tension is built up into the chassis.

A racecar will use shocks, springs, dampeners, sway bars and track bars to help dial in the handling. A shifter kart uses track width, axle stiffness, axle hub length, seat struts, etc. to achieve this same affect.

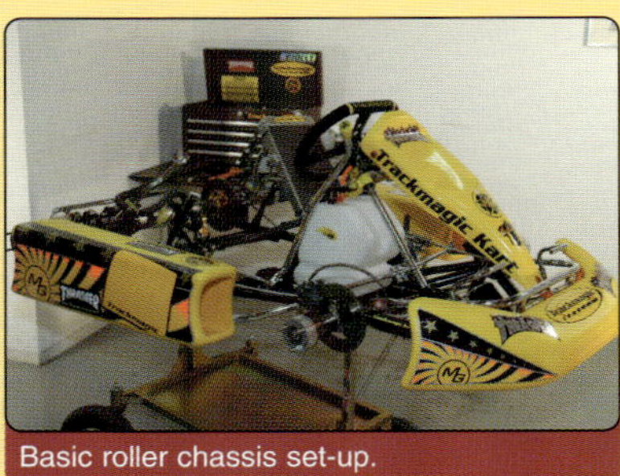
Basic roller chassis set-up.

How a shifter kart works

This makes the set-up of each component on the kart very critical. The main force to be looked at is weight transfer. This transfer of weight from one tire to another is by design and will influence the handling of a kart in many different ways. Other factors to be considered include track width, center of gravity and track conditions.

Front End

The role of the front end of the kart is to control the direction and stability of the kart at speed. With 125's the front must also do this under intense braking. The geometry built into the frame and spindles causes a weight jacking effect, which helps the inside rear wheel to lift. The most important element of the front-end design is commonly referred to as King Pin Inclination (KPI) and is designed by the chassis manufacturer based on the engine type and its intended use. It is the KPI that not only causes the inside front wheel to drop and the outside front wheel to rise in relation to each other, but also affects the attitude of the tire to the track surface. The KPI is made up of caster and camber, two different angles that work together to help a kart change direction quickly and efficiently.

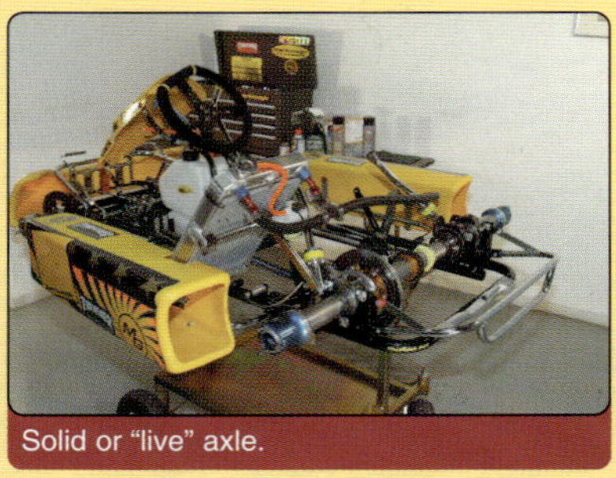
Solid or "live" axle.

The first and most important angle is the caster angle or the rearward angle that the front spindle has in relation to vertical or plumb. A kart will never have zero caster (vertical) or negative caster (forward lean) as this will not allow the weight jacking to occur. All karts have positive caster built into them through the positioning of the spindle yoke welded to the chassis. As more caster angle is applied, the more weight jacking effect will occur on the kart.

Proper king pin and spindle setup.

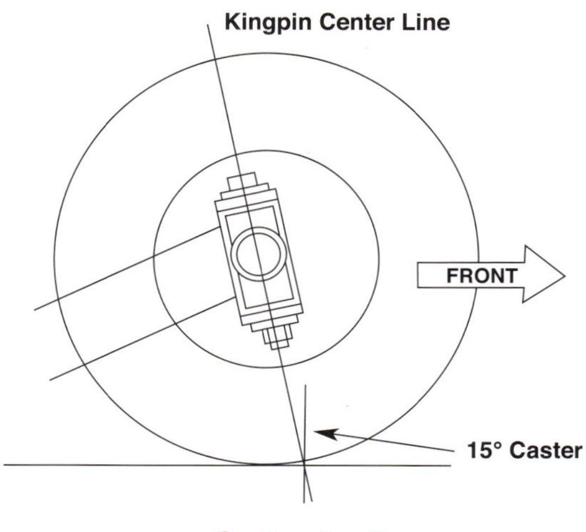

Caster Angle

Notice camber angle of king pin.

The second angle is the camber angle or the inward angle that the King Pin has in relation to plumb. All karts have some camber built into the spindle yoke. However, much of this angle is removed in the design of the spindle stub axle, leaving zero camber on most karts. This allows the tire to be flat to the racing surface providing maximum grip. Camber angle changes will affect the attitude of the tires to the track surface during cornering and straight line driving, along with affecting the weight jacking characteristics.

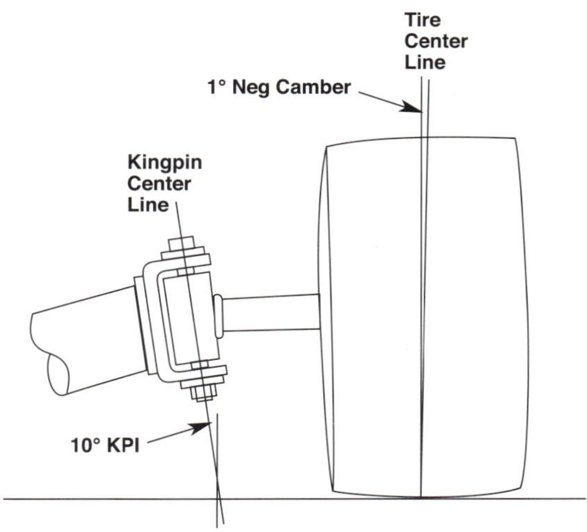

Camber Angle

Caster pill with four settings.

Both camber and caster can be added or removed using special "pills" or bushings, which are set into the top of the yoke where the spindle bolt goes through. The pill has an offset hole, usually at specific degrees from center. As the pill is rotated to the outside, caster is removed and negative camber is added. As the pill is turned inward, again the caster is removed and this time positive camber is added. These pills can be rotated a full 360 degrees, having varying effects on the chassis.

Ackerman steering setup.

Rear Axle layout.

Rear wheel axle hub.

80cc front spindle set up.

125cc front spindle set up.

Toe Angle is the relationship of the front tires to each other. Zero-toe means that the wheels are parallel to each other. Toe-in or negative toe means that the tires point in toward each other. Toe-out, also called positive toe, means that the tires point away from each other. We will deal with the effects of toe in chapter eight.

Ackerman has an effect on the front wheels as the steering is turned. It uses the angle of the spindle arms and offset holes on the steering shaft to make the inner wheel turn more than the outer wheel. This causes the inside front wheel to turn on a tighter radius than the outside front tire, which reduces the tire scrub while corning. Along with this, adding Ackerman will also increase the weight jacking effect, and help the weight transfer.

Rear End

The role of the rear of the kart is to deliver power and accelerate the kart forward. This may sound obvious, but being able to get the power to the ground is a critical element to shifter kart performance. We will look at axles, bearings and hubs to see how they work together to control flex of the axle and maintain traction through a corner.

There are a number of different axle lengths, diameters and thicknesses to choose from which can be combined with a number of different hub lengths. The end result is all the same, controlling the flex of the axle to provide the perfect amount of inside wheel lift and compliancy. Just like the suspension on a motocross bike helps to absorb the bumps and get the wheels back to the ground quickly, the axle on a shifter kart will do much the same. The quicker the turn can be completed and both wheels firmly planted on the track, the quicker the horsepower can be delivered to the ground with the result being better traction.

The back end of a shifter kart tends to be wider, but does not differ much from a traditional kart. The most critical area of the back of the kart is where the axle is located. The axle is mounted on bearings, which sit inside bearing cassettes. These cassettes are in turn bolted to hangers. There are a couple of different hanger styles in use today. They can adjust the ride height and wheelbase by providing different alignment holes or positioning bushings.

The role of the bearing cassette is to hold the bearing firmly, yet allow the frame rails to move and twist with minimal friction. The bearings allow the axle to rotate freely and allow the chassis to flex. We will talk about axles in greater detail later in this chapter.

The Chassis

The role of the chassis is to join the input from each end and provide just the right amount of flex or resistance to achieve optimum turning and bump absorbing performance. There are a number of components that can be clamped onto a chassis to help manage this flex. The purpose of these bars are to stiffen the chassis. These bars are especially helpful in a shifter kart because the extra horsepower and speed increase the forces applied to the chassis.

Key Components

In this section we will look at the many components that come together to create a shifter kart. Every component has a major impact on the handling of the kart and must be dealt with individually.

Spindles and Front Hubs

The front spindles and hubs on a shifter kart are similar in design to traditional karts, but with more radical King Pin Inclination in order to jack more weight. Most 80cc karts run the standard spindle/stub axle configuration. The bearing can either be on a hub or built into the front wheel. This type of front spindle uses a series of small spacers to move the spindle in or out, to change front track width.

The spindles on 125cc shifter karts tend to be heavier in construction and carry brackets to support the brake calipers. There are two types of front hub assemblies to accommodate the brake rotor. One uses an outer axle that fits over the stub axle and is fixed in place. You then slide a hub over the outer axle to make track width adjustments possible. The other version is a fixed outer axle that uses spacers over the wheel studs to move the track width in or out.

Padded steering wheel for good grip.

Steering System

There are many different styles of wheels and clutch lever systems. Some systems bolt to the side of the steering wheel hub and pull on the outer casing. Another style of clutch lever clamps to the top of the steering column, much like a lever on a dirt bike, and pulls from the top. There are angled steering wheel hubs, which can change the pitch of the steering wheel, making hand position more comfortable.

Tie rods are what connect the spindles to the steering column. The hemispherical joints help make steering smooth and easy. Keeping the front end steering smooth and free from binding is important for consistent driving. It is recommended that a light lubricant be used on the hemispherical joints.

Bump shift assembly.

Shifters

There are two types of shifter choices when buying a kart: butterfly style or bump style. Both have certain pros and cons and really it comes down to driver comfort and preference.

A paddle type shifter allows the driver to keep both hands on the wheel all the time. An obvious benefit is that steering is more consistent. The downside of a butterfly shifter is that the shifting is a little slower and not quite as direct due to the push/pull style cable attached to the shift arm and lever.

Bump shifters, on the other hand, are usually attached solidly with an aluminum rod, which makes shifting very precise and direct. However, many times with a bump shifter you will be using only one hand to steer in the corners as you are downshifting with the other. This makes the steering a little harder to control.

If you are a new driver or don't get to the track that often I would recommend a butterfly style shifter. If you kart quite a bit then a bump shifter is the way to go. I prefer the bump shifter because it puts my hand in a position on the steering wheel that gives me the best leverage. Either way, you always want to make sure that your system is smooth and does not bind. This means no excessive kinks or bends in the cable or rod, which will make the shifting harder. It is always amazing to me the number of karts I see that have shifting that is extremely hard because of cable or line routing. Getting your shifting mechanisms to work properly is free time on the racetrack.

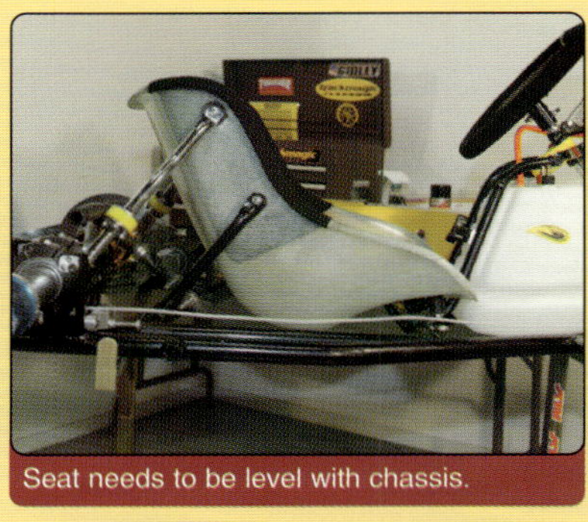
Seat needs to be level with chassis.

Front brakes can be cross drilled.

Seat

One of the most significant components on a kart is the seat. In a racecar the seat is critical to driver safety and must be custom fitted to ensure maximum protection. In a kart the seat is a performance component and has a direct impact on the drivability of a kart. This is so important we have dedicated an entire chapter to the installation of the seat. We will explore the seat and its affect on the kart in more detail in chapter four.

Brakes

The use of brakes in the front is one of the more important differences with a shifter kart over other karting. This, combined with the bigger tire, provides incredible stopping capabilities. Most top-level shifter karts use fully vented rotors to help control any excessive temperature. The use of separate master cylinders is a significant safety feature and makes the systems more adaptable between 80cc and 125cc configurations. Many of the brake systems are twin caliper allowing for incredible stopping power. The rear brake caliper and rotor tend to be bigger on shifter karts than traditional karts because of the extra weight of the shifter kart.

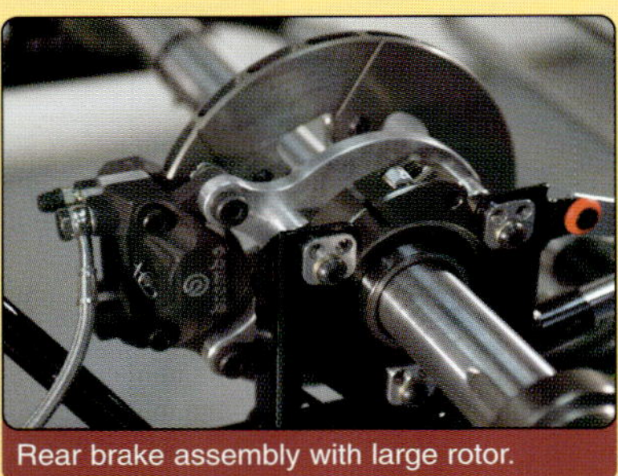
Rear brake assembly with large rotor.

Rear Axle

The important thing to remember is that however stiff the axle appears to be, it does and will flex. Not only does the axle flex between the bearing and wheel hub, but also considerable flex or bowing happens in the middle of the frame between the bearings. The longer the "clear" axle segment is, the more the axle will flex. Changes like the length of hubs or the width of the rear track can change this distance. With the axle itself, the softer the axle material the more it will flex and the thinner the axle wall the more it will flex.

Again, the important thing when picking the right axle is to try to match the stiffness with the amount of grip and/or bumps of the track that you are driving. Generally, you want to load the tire as hard (stiff) as possible without collapsing the sidewall to the point that it acts like an un-dampened spring and the kart begins to hop.

Proper rear bearing installation.

Rear Wheel Hubs

There are three main hub lengths from which to choose, including 75mm, 100mm and 125mm. There is a special 50mm for rain, which will be discussed in chapter 11. As you increase the hub length you reduce the flex of the axle. The hubs are generally machined from billet aluminum or cast magnesium. Adjusting track width will change axle flex. The wider the rear track, the more leverage the wheels have, and the softer the axle will act.

Three different rear hub lengths.

Torsion Bars

A torsion bar can be added to the back, side or front of a shifter kart. It is usually clamped in place between the outermost rails with removable clamps. The net effect is to stiffen or soften the chassis by controlling the amount of flex.

The most common torsion bar is at the rear of the kart. The rear torsion bar is also called a blade because it is pressed flat in the middle section. The rear torsion bar is clamped in place between the outside frame rails at the back of the chassis. The bar can be rotated to provide varying degrees of torsional stiffness.

The front axle is the same as the rear torsion bar only mounted across the front, in line with the spindle yokes. In most cases this is a removable bar that is held in place with clamps. These clamps can be tightened or loosened to provide varying degrees of torsional stiffness. Along with adjusting the frame flex between the two wheels, the front torsion bar has a huge effect on the weight jacking characteristics of the kart. The bar in, the kart will jack more weight while the bar is out, the front end will be less responsive.

Many karts have a fourth rail that runs along the left side of the chassis and is clamped in place between the forward cross member and the rear cross member. This component has much of the same effect as the rear torsion bar.

Cooling System

The cooling system really brings in a new dimension to the set-up of a traditional kart. The hoses are mounted across the kart and can come in contact with many different components. For the first time, we are adding a substantial component and weight to the left side of the kart. The cooling system is critical in keeping the engine at optimal temperature, ensuring maximum performance.

Mounting is very important and the radiator needs to be well secured to avoid excessive vibration, which can crack the core. Insulating the radiator from the chassis and vice versa is very important. Placement of the hoses and lines should be well planned to ensure that the flow is smooth and that nothing gets pinched. The flow of the water hoses should be very natural.

Clamps need to be checked often. The best types of hose clamps have a smooth inner steel lining that will not chew up the rubber hose. Good quality clamps will ensure the hoses stay firmly in place. Remember, the pump can clear the system of coolant in a few seconds, leaving very little time to react before overheating occurs.

I always recommend that you have, at a minimum, a head temperature sensor on your kart. This is because head temperature will tell you immediately if there is a problem with your cooling system. Personally, I run both a head temperature and water temperature sensor at all times, to get the most accurate picture of how my cooling system is working.

Remember, just as it's possible to seize your engine by getting it too hot, you can also seize your engine if it runs too cold. This is called a cold siezure. Also, not warming your engine and immediately gassing it will cause excessive wear on the internals of the engine.

Different engines use different style water pumps. The ICC style engines use an external pump, which consists of a frame mounted pump and a drive gear with a belt driven off of the rear axle. Most of the maintenance is keeping the right amount of tension and proper alignment of the belt. Most belts or O-rings need to have just a slight tension on them to keep the pump spinning at all times. If the belt breaks, you will need to remove the entire axle assembly to replace it. For this reason, have a spare belt mounted to the rear axle ready to use at a moments notice. Moto style engines use the internal pump stock on all models.

Both style pumps should be taken apart regularly when the

Transverse front torsion bar.

Fourth rail torsion bar.

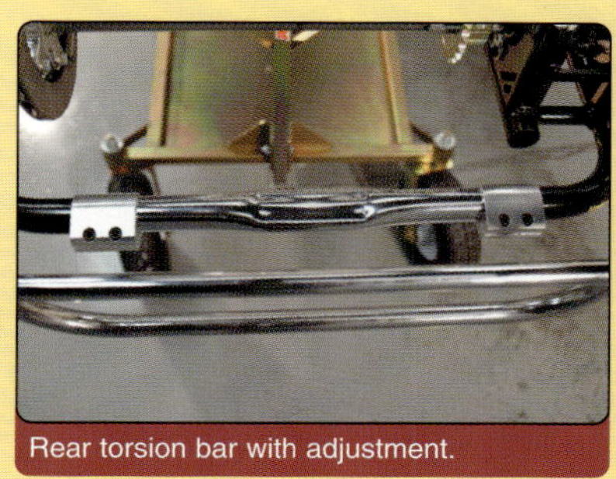

Rear torsion bar with adjustment.

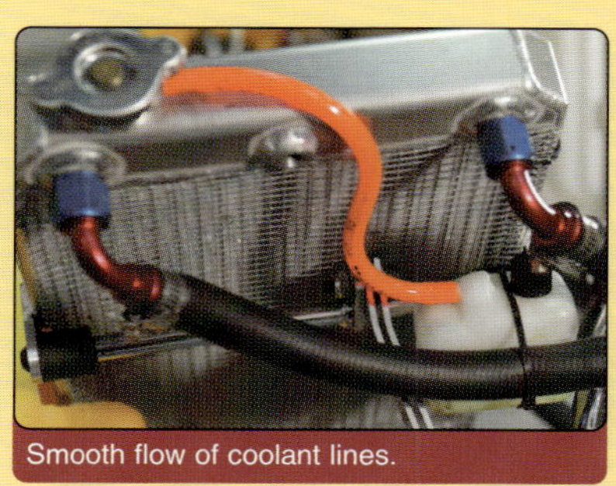

Smooth flow of coolant lines.

ICC external water pump.

Moto engine internal water pump.

Loosening the rear brake rotor.

cool trick

Some brake rotor hubs are very hard to loosen up even with the bolt removed. Take the bolt and thread it in the opposite side. Place a hard washer into the split area. As you tighten the bolt against the washer it will push the rotor apart just enough to keep it loose.

engine is completely rebuilt to inspect for any excessive impeller or seal wear. I recommend that a "water wetter" type cooling treatment be used when mixing the water. Along with temperature and anti-freezing benefits, these treatments have a lubricant for the seals, which will add considerably to the trouble free performance of your pump.

Whenever the water solution in the radiator is drained and replaced, proper air removal in the radiator and lines is critical. As discussed earlier, the best procedure I've found is, after filling your radiator, tip the kart on its side for a few seconds in order to make the filler cap of the radiator the highest point. As we all know, air rises to the top. When you place the kart horizontal again, check to see if the level of coolant in the radiator has dropped. Continue with this procedure until the water level remains consistent. This usually takes between two and three times.

Rear Axle Removal and Installation

Most components on your kart are mounted in a very straightforward manner. The only areas that really carry any mystery and require some real care and consideration before installing are the rear axle and bearings. The rear axle of the kart is critical to the overall performance of the kart. As we learned earlier in this chapter, the axle moves and flexes with the chassis.

The axle fits inside three separate roller bearings, each of which is mounted into a cassette. The design of the bearing and the cassette allows the bearing to rotate, which works with the chassis flex. Each bearing has a short side and a long side. The long side is drilled and tapped to hold a setscrew. This allows the axle to firmly connect to the bearing. The cassettes sit into a mounting hanger that is welded to the frame. The hanger usually has two to three holes that allow for adjusting the ride height of the kart.

To remove the axle, remove the wheels and the hubs. Next remove the chain and drive gear. Some cassettes split in half, which allows you to slide the axle out with the bearings and brake rotor in place. Most require you to pull the axle out. First loosen the brake rotor hub. This is usually just one big bolt. Some brake rotor hubs have a tiny setscrew. Make sure you loosen this or it will mark the axle surface as you try to pull out the axle.

Remove the setscrews from the bearings. Before you begin to pull the axle, try to turn each bearing to ensure it does not stick. Also, wipe off the entire surface of the axle with WD40. Pull from either side. You may need to use a rubber mallet or a urethane axle remover. Never hit the axle with a metal hammer. Once you have moved the axle three to four inches, stop and wipe off the area that was covered by the bearing or the rotor hub. Again, use WD40 to help remove the grit. The axle should slide out very easily.

Once the axle is out, begin by inspecting it for any burrs or marks. Use a fine file to remove burrs, especially around the key way slots. Also, use fine sandpaper or steel wool to remove any rust or marks on the axle surface. Finally, use a fine Scotch Brite pad and a little WD40 to polish the axle. This will ensure that the axle will slide nicely into the bearings.

Clean all the bearings with a dry rag and check that they spin freely without any tight spots or noticeable grit lodged inside. I would not attempt to clean the bearings in a solvent tank and re-use them. The reason is that solvent tanks are usually full of small metal particles and dirt that can get trapped in the bearings. It's usually best just to buy a new set of bearings if they appear gritty or are in marginal condition.

Since the bearings and bearing cassettes are out of the frame, this is a great time to thoroughly clean the back of the frame with a rag and a little WD40. Bathroom style cotton swabs work great for those hard to reach places like in the corners of the bearing hangers welded to the frame.

The installation of the axle is probably one of the most critical areas of kart performance. An improperly installed axle will rob the engine of horsepower and make the kart handle poorly. It is important that all of the axle parts are clean and free of all burrs before beginning the installation process. Before we concern ourselves with installing the drive gear, brake rotor or water pump pulley, we must first make sure that the bearings are lined up in the frame. This will only be correct if we can have all the bearing cassettes tight in the frame while still being able to slide the axle freely through them.

First, apply a very light coat of anti-seize to the inside of the cassettes and install the bearings. Then install the three cassettes into the kart and tighten just slightly snug. Now try to slide your axle through. If the axle won't go in, gently tap on the cassettes and the axle with a rubber mallet. I always line up the outer two cassettes first and then attempt to align the inside third bearing before fully tightening the cassette bolts. When the axle is in all the way, spin and tap lightly with a rubber mallet to complete the bearing alignment. Tighten each cassette and tap the axle as you go.

When all the cassettes are tight you should be able to spin the axle with ease. Now slide the axle back out of the two right side bearings and slip on the water pump gear, drive gear, axle collars and brake rotor hub. Slide the axle back through the bearings. Push the axle just far enough so you can put the brake rotor key way in place. Push the axle back and align it evenly on both sides. Tighten the setscrews or the axle collars. Some karters use axle collars instead of the traditional setscrews to secure the axle from sliding. The benefit of using collars is that they do not leave marks or mar the axle like setscrews. However, it is important to make sure that the collars do not slide on the axle and that they remain tight.

Sometimes, no matter how hard you try, the bearings won't line up and the axle will not slide through. This is usually because the bearing hangers on the frame are not perfectly aligned. If this is the case, drill out the cassette holes in the third bearing to allow for extra clearance. Although this is not ideal, it is much better than just tightening down the misaligned cassettes, which will preload the bearings and cause drag and poor handling.

Base Line

With all the information you have learned about setting up a shifter kart, where do you begin? I would recommend that you talk with the manufacturer of your brand of kart to find out a starting set-up. The dealer should ask you questions like your body size and weight, your height, the track you plan to run on, the tires you have on your kart, and which engine you are running. If they don't ask you those types of specific questions then they really won't be able to give you a starting set-up.

Filing off burrs on the key way.

Use anti-sieze on the bearing cassettes.

hot tip

I always use a thin layer of anti-seize compound between the aluminum cassette and the steel bearing. This will ensure smooth sliding between the two surfaces without any galling or binding of the two materials.

Spin and tap the axle to set the bearings.

hot tip

It is recommended that steel collars be used. They tend not to grow with heat like aluminum collars, therefore keeping the axle from sliding.

Steel axle collars hold the axle in place.

hot tip

Clean the part of the axle where the axle collars will sit with brake or contact cleaner before you install them. This will ensure they do not move or slip.

Making sure axle is even.

In either case, I would recommend that you start somewhere on the safe or easy to drive side. This means not a lot of caster or positive camber, keep the front end on the narrow side, the rear end on the wide side, and mount the seat so that it has room to be adjusted forward or backwards and not too upright. These settings should keep the kart fairly stable. As far as axle stiffness, hubs, bars etc., I would recommend that you start with settings that allow you to tune on both sides. Meaning, if you have a choice of axles, install the middle stiffness and so on. Remember, consistency with your kart and your driving should be the first goal.

Maintenance – Keeping it Clean

One of the more important things you can do for your kart is to keep it clean. Obviously this is important to every kart and especially true in shifter karts because of the extra components and the additional force. I live by the saying "A clean kart is a happy kart and a happy kart is a fast kart." The idea being that anything mechanical operates better when properly maintained and cleaned. This eliminates possible problems and helps you discover loose bolts or damaged parts before they become a problem and lose you a race.

Start by blowing off all the dirt and dust you can. Be careful when using compressed air. Always wear safety glasses when using an air hose. Next take a rag and lightly coat it with WD40. This will help cut through the grease and grime on your kart and help to keep rust from forming on any bare metal surfaces. I usually start with the front of the kart, which is usually the cleanest, and work my way back. The chain area is the last spot to clean.

It is a good idea to remove the wheels and clean the hubs and rims. Use this opportunity to check the studs, rims, bolts and tires for damage. Don't be afraid to pull off the hubs and give them a quick cleaning. Make sure you take width measurements before you pull them off. Most hub problems come from grit and grease getting in between the hub and the axle, either causing them to slip or be difficult to adjust. Make sure you give each surface a quick shot of brake cleaner before you put them back on. Your hubs should move easily when loosened and be solidly in place when tight. Put the wheels back on and tighten the stud bolts firmly.

Another area to keep clean is the rear axle. With a chain and chain lube, this area can be a real mess. The grease flies everywhere and then attracts grit. Start with a clean rag and remove as much as possible. Use WD40 to loosen and remove the stubborn grease on the bearings, axle and rear gear. Using WD40 ensures that you lubricate at the same time as you clean. Clean the entire rear end, including the bumper, the frame, bearings and the cassettes, by putting some WD40 on a rag and polishing the surface. This makes the next cleaning even easier.

Properly working brakes are important and you should take the time to maintain them and check for any problem areas. Start with a dry rag and remove as much dust and grime as possible. Clean in and around the rotor hub and the caliper themselves. Use a good quality brake cleaner. Take the nozzle hose and spray into the brake caliper. This should force any brake dust or track grit out. Don't be afraid to use the cleaner, as it dries with no residue. Try not to soak the pad itself.

Another area to keep clean is the engine. I start at the top of the engine using contact cleaner and compressed air. Again, for those areas with heavy grease, a toothbrush along with contact cleaner and compressed air works great. Don't go crazy with the contact cleaner and make sure to keep away from all painted surfaces. If you have run off course and picked up a lot of dirt, don't forget to remove the tank bolt and clean underneath the fuel tank. The grit in between the floor pan and the fuel tank can act like sandpaper and wear on both the plastic tank bottom and the aluminum surface of the floor pan.

After a race day you should pull the engine for a more thorough cleaning. Remove the engine and place it on your bench. Before you begin place a clean piece of shop towel or cloth into the exhaust port and the intake flange to make sure nothing gets into the engine while you are cleaning it. Wipe off everything and make sure you clean all the electronic parts. Wipe off the chassis where the engine mount sits and also wipe off the side of the seat. This usually gets covered in grime. Clean the engine mount thoroughly, including the brackets that go underneath. You want a nice, clean contact between the engine mount and the chassis to ensure the engine does not move.

Another part that gets overlooked is the steering column support bracket. This is a friction fit area and can collect a lot of grit. Remove the bracket bolt and slip the bracket up the steering shaft. Wipe off the column and put back in place with a little WD40 for good measure. Make sure to wait a few minutes before reinstalling so all of the WD40 can run through.

And lastly, the finishing touch to a clean kart is the bodywork. If the bodywork is relatively clean the process is simple. I take a clean rag and spray it and the bodywork with WD40. WD40 works great to loosen all the stained grease and will not smear and ruin your stickers. Never use brake or carb cleaner. Not only will they ruin your stickers, but they will also dry out and fade your bodywork. After the bodywork is free of all grease, take another clean rag and clean with Simple Green style cleaner. This will give the plastic that non-greasy look and help to keep dust and dirt from building up on the surface.

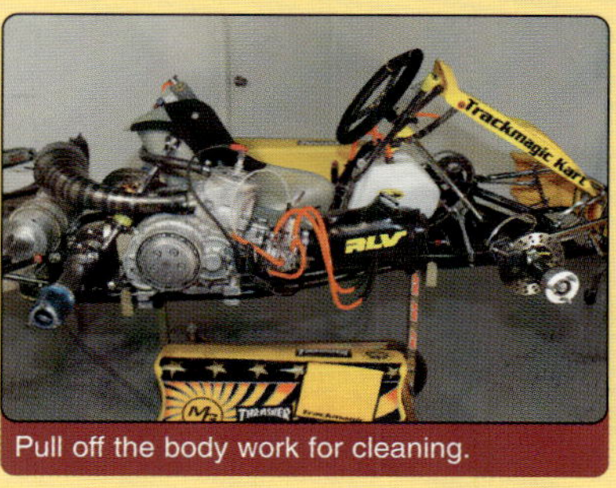

Pull off the body work for cleaning.

cool trick

The other process that works even better to clean the bodywork is using a soapy/warm water solution, similar to what you would use to wash your car. After removing and cleaning the bodywork with WD40, use the soapy solution and soft wash mitt to remove all the stubborn stains and rubber marks. Do one piece at a time and immediately rinse with clean water from a hose. Using a towel immediately after to dry the bodywork will help to replenish any lost moisture back into the plastic and help it to keep its shine.

hot tip

Never use Scotch Brite to scrub the bodywork as extreme fading will occur and the plastic will loose all of its shine.

SEAT SET-UP

Notice the seat is left of center.

Seat Dynamics 101

The seat is one of the most critical components of a shifter kart because it's the seat that connects the largest mass, you the driver, to the kart. Many articles have been written about just how important the seat is to the set-up and to the handling of a shifter kart. This is because too often the seat is improperly positioned or poorly installed, directly affecting the handling performance of the chassis. This is especially true in shifters because, as we discussed in chapter three, everything happens to a greater degree in a shifter kart. In this chapter we will de-mystify the seat and make sure you get it right the first time.

The seat can control the weight transfer, center of gravity, chassis flex and weight balance. A properly installed seat will complement these forces, while a poorly installed seat will work against the chassis, causing a number of handling problems. A well-installed and properly fitted seat means seconds a lap.

Like the geometry and flex built into the chassis, kart manufacturers spend a lot of time on seat positioning. Most manufacturers will have recommended settings for optimum performance. These are available from your dealer or from the manufacturer's website. You should always consult your chassis manufacturer or your seat manufacturer for exact mounting specifications. Later in this chapter we will provide some seat set-up guidelines, which should be compared to your manufacturer's specifications.

hot tip

A proper fitting seat keeps the driver comfortable, reducing fatigue, injury and allowing for proper steering input.

The first step to installing the seat properly is to ensure that you do not pre-load the chassis with tension. If the bolts are out of alignment or the seat has to be pulled or twisted into place, it will put pressure and tension on the chassis before the kart even gets rolling. This will greatly affect the flex and the tuning consistency of the kart.

When installing your seat you need to look at driver size, track conditions, tire type and engine style. The position of the seat can be adjusted to ensure maximum performance from each of these elements. Drivers must learn that like tires, the seat is a commodity that gets consumed. Top drivers will change seats regularly to keep the handling performance consistent. This is especially relevant to North American drivers who may run street races during which the seat can hit the ground, sustaining significant damage.

Seat should be centered and level.

How a kart seat works

As we mentioned earlier, the seat will affect the transfer of weight, the flex of the chassis, the overall balance of the kart and the center of gravity. All of these help pick up the inside rear wheel, which is required to help the kart turn through a corner. The cause and effect that the seat produces has a major impact on the directional stability of the kart under braking and through cornering.

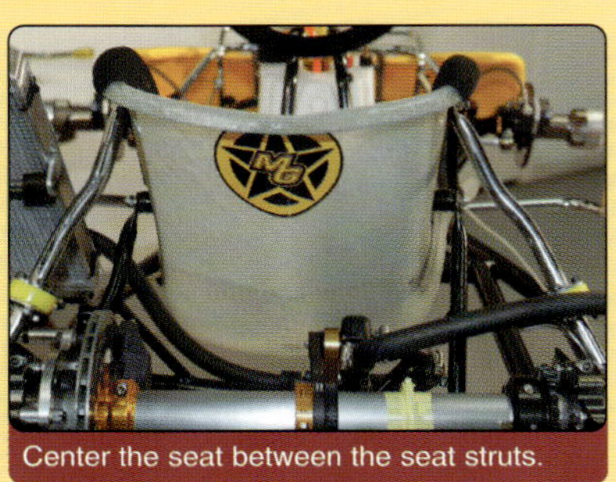

Center the seat between the seat struts.

From chapter three we learned of the geometry built into a chassis to create weight transfer. As the geometry of the chassis affects weight transfer, the seat can add to this by transferring more or less of the driver's mass. The force applied by the driver as the kart is changing direction enhances this weight transfer as the driver's body pushes outward on the seat when the kart turns through a corner. We can use the seat to control how much of this energy is transferred. A loose or incorrectly fitted seat can create unnecessary transfer of weight and throw off the balance of the kart. The weight of the driver can "slosh," if the seat is not bolted properly or the seat is too big for the driver.

Much like torsion bars affect frame flex, the seat can add to the torsional flex. Kart seats are manufactured using resin-based composites like fiberglass and carbon fiber to create a shell that is shaped to hold a driver firmly in place. Different materials are used to create a range of torsional stiffnesses and weights. Varying the stiffness of the seat directly affects how much or how quickly your body loads the frame and/or tires on your kart.

We know that ride height affects the center of gravity. The seat height can also be used to control how high the center of gravity is set. The center of gravity of a kart starts off low to begin with. However, add in the driver and now a large mass is positioned very high. The seat can be used to adjust this critical point, which can amplify the weight transfer and inside rear wheel pick up on the entry to the corner and tire loading on the exit.

Finally, we will use the seat to make major changes to the balance of the kart.

By moving the seat forward you can take weight from the back to the front. By moving the seat to the left of center you can offset the weight of the engine. We will go into a detailed description of kart balancing in chapter eight.

Use proper mounting washers.

warning

Always use the proper mounting washers on your seat. I recommend using hard plastic type washers. It is extremely important that the two mounting surfaces, the seat and the strut, are aligned properly and parallel to keep the seat from cracking when being tightened.

Key Components

The design of a kart seat is very basic and similar from manufacturer to manufacturer. A kart seat needs to support the driver in cornering, acceleration and deceleration. In a racecar, the driver is belted in, while in a kart the seat is cupped to hold the driver from behind, from the sides and from the front. A good seat should hold the driver firmly and support the hips. Most seats will have a spine relief in the form of a groove down the back to keep pressure off the driver's spine, making it more comfortable. Some seats have a hole drilled in the bottom to drain water when racing in the rain. Also, you can find seats that have holes down the back to provide air circulation.

Seats can be purchased fully padded, partially padded or not padded at all. Padding on a seat becomes important in shifter karts as they are heavier and more voilent and the forces from accelerating and braking are much greater than traditional karts.

Mounting Supports

The front mounting tabs are welded to the first cross member, just behind the fuel tank and usually in line with the steering column supports. They are generally positioned about five to six inches apart, or the width of the fuel tank. This keeps the front of the seat in position and provides a solid attachment point.

The side mounting supports hold the seat in place from both the left and the right side. These supports are attached to the side rails and to the rear cross rail as well. Some chassis manufacturers use a right side support that can be clamped on, allowing you to position it where it fits best. Again, the manufacturer defines much of this.

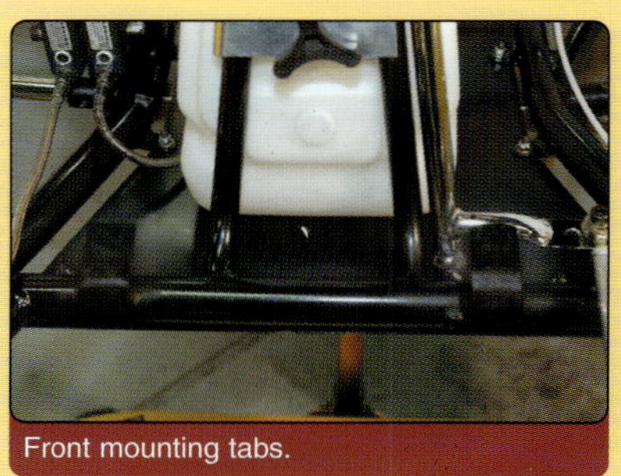
Front mounting tabs.

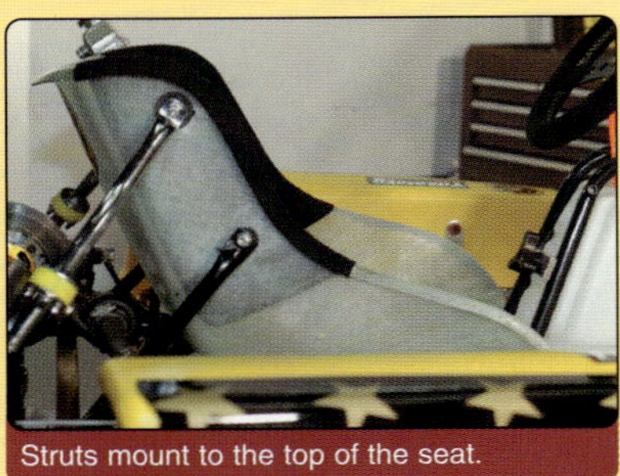
Struts mount to the top of the seat.

Set a board under the chassis.

hot tip

To bend the seat strut to the desired position, try using an old 40mm axle. It will slide right over the strut and provide enough leverage to easily bend the strut where you want it. Be careful to bend slowly, moving the axle up the strut with every little bend so that you don't kink the strut.

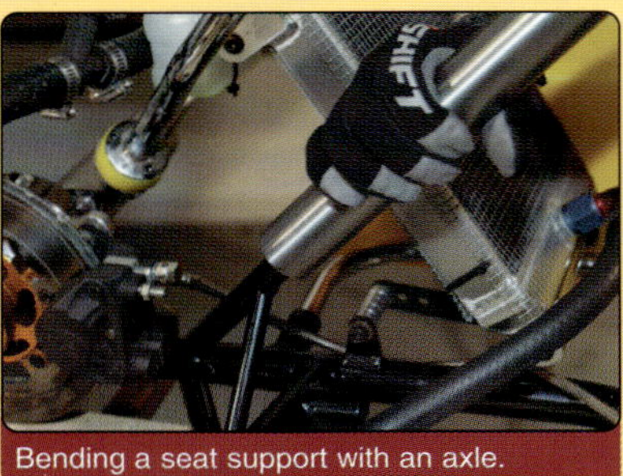

Bending a seat support with an axle.

Seat Struts

Most seat struts are made from tube steel with the ends flattened to allow for flush mounting. Some are made from round stock while others use flat tubing. Trackmagic has developed a unique strut that uses a urethane spacer in the middle that can be adjusted for flex.

Seat struts are extremely important to the overall performance of the seat and the kart. It is through the struts that the weight transfer from the driver is connected to the rear wheels. Loosen or remove the struts and the weight transfer effect will diminish. In chapter 10 and 11, when we look at race set-up, the issue of struts will come up often.

Installation

In this section we will go into the process of seat installation and attempt to anticipate some factors that you may encounter while installing or repositioning your seat. Before you begin you will need to get your tools together. You will need a drill, preferably cordless, a 15/64" (6mm) drill bit for the M6 bolts and a 5/16" (8mm) drill for M8 bolts. Also, you will need M13 and M10 wrenches, along with T4 and T5 hex head sockets or T-handles.

Make sure you have the proper hardware before you get started. All the nuts need to be Nylock style so they do not vibrate loose. The bolts should be the countersunk or flat head variety. These bolts use a special washer that makes for a smooth surface on the seat and distributes the pressure over a wider area to prevent cracking around the bolt holes.

Start by putting your kart up on the stand. Next, clamp a six inch wide piece of plywood under the frame from side to side just forward of the seat side supports. Spring clamps work great; be careful not to scratch the chassis finish. Make sure that there are no tye wraps, engine mounts or struts in the way. Have a couple of pieces of 1/8th inch stock on hand. These shims may be placed under the rails, lowering the board, if you are a tall driver, not used at all if you are medium height and placed on top of the board, raising the seat, if you are short.

Set the seat in place and center it between the side seat posts. If there are excessive gaps on each side bring the side supports closer together. You will need a long pipe that can go over the seat support or fit in between the support and the side rail to bend it back. Remember, you do not need to move the pipe very much to move the support.

The seat spacers can be made from aluminum or hard plastic. Never use soft rubber spacers as they split apart when being tightened. Edge cracks in the seat are common, when seats are mounted with spacers made of an extremely flexible material like rubber. It is important to use the same type of spacers for both sides. This will keep the seat mounting symmetrical and help the kart to work the same in both left and right turns.

Two important angles must now be considered in mounting your seat. They are the lean angle and the offset angle. Let's look at the lean angle first. According to Tillett Racing Seats, the flat area on the base of the seat will determine the angle for the seat. Also, you can use 33° from vertical, as this is the angle most experienced drivers sit at. In terms of the offset angle, the seat should be mounted slightly towards the left rear in order to offset the weight of the engine. Keep in mind that the back lip of the seat should always be forward of the axle. For your seat baseline, the top of the seat should be level in order to keep your body square in the kart.

Ensure that the distance between the seat and the tank on the left and right sides are relatively the same. Mark the holes of the side supports, remove the seat and drill the boltholes. These will be M8 bolts, so use your 8mm or 5/16" drill bit. Set the seat back in place and bolt in the side supports. As you tighten listen for cracking of the seat. If necessary, add a couple of washers to snug the fit. If the gap is larger than 1/2", pull the seat out and bring the side supports in closer together an equal amount from each side.

With the side bolts in place you are ready to mark the front support tab bolts. Lift the front of the seat up and place the bolts for the front supports with a couple of spacers into the mounting tabs. Do not include the top mounting washer. Tighten the nuts to hold the bolts firmly in place. Set the seat back down and let it rest on the head of the bolts. Check to see if they make equal contact.

You may need to add or take away a spacer, making sure the seat is resting evenly on the mounts. This step can take some time playing with the spacers to get the distance setting right. You may have more spacers on one side do to the offset of the seat. If one bolt seems to angle differently from the seat, the tabs can be moved up or down to get the proper alignment. Use a large adjustable wrench to move the tabs up or down. Remember, a little movement at the end of the wrench is a big change in the angle of the tab.

With the heads of the bolts in contact with the bottom of the seat, you should now be able to see the head of the bolt through the seat. Mark the center of the bolts from the top, lift the seat and drill the holes.

Remove the bolts from the tabs, put the seat washers in place, put the spacers back in place and push the bolt through the tab. Put on the nuts and tighten. Again, listen for cracking as you tighten the bolts. If you hear any cracking, adjust the tabs to allow the bolts to slide in easily.

Mounting auxiliary seat struts is a critical component of the entire seat mounting process. It is through the struts that the majority of the weight transfer happens. The struts take the energy from the seat and transfer it to the rear wheels. This principle is very important to understand when mounting seat struts. Never bend seat struts to fit around components of your kart like the carburetor or air filter. There are adaptors and accessories you can purchase to make sure that these components do not interfere with the struts. A bent strut on one side of the kart will not transfer the same energy that a non-bent strut on the other side will, thus creating inconsistent handling.

First, select the appropriate length of strut by measuring from the bearing cassette holder to the top outside of the seat. Put the strut in place to see how the mounting tabs sit against the cassette and the seat. Bend the end tabs in or out to get a nice flush fit. Install the bottom bolt at the cassette and finger tighten. Place the strut at the appropriate angle and mark a hole on the seat. Move the strut and drill the hole as marked. Install the top bolt and tighten. Listen for cracking in the seat. Many karts will require two struts. The second strut should be mounted in the forward position and run parallel to the first strut.

Again, ensure all fasteners are tight. What you have done is made the seat neutral at this point. You have just completed the most important job in ensuring your chassis will perform up to its potential.

Mark the holes before drilling.

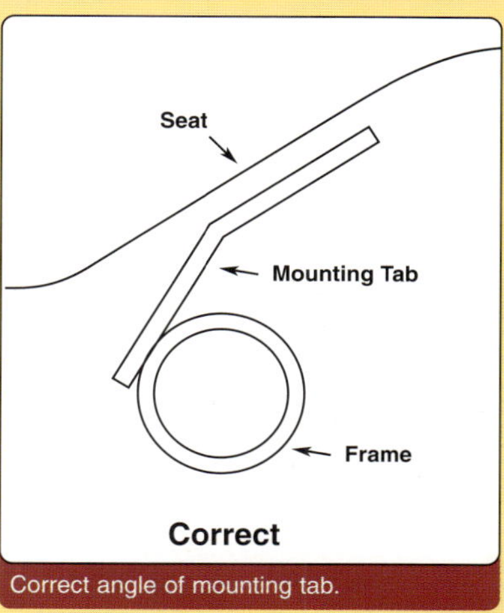

Correct angle of mounting tab.

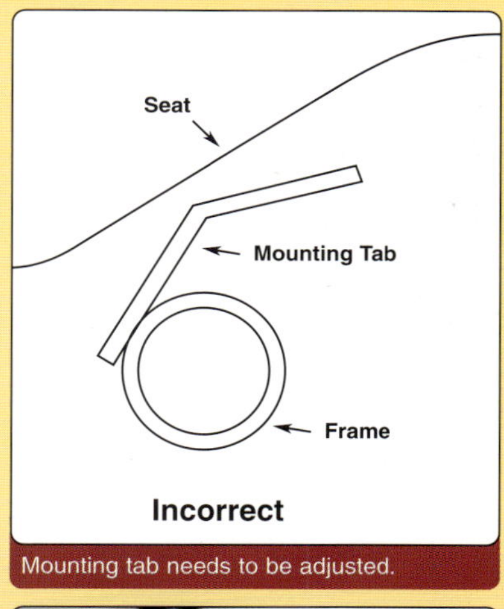

Mounting tab needs to be adjusted.

Front tab mounting hardware.

Mark the hole from above.

Always use proper mounting washers.

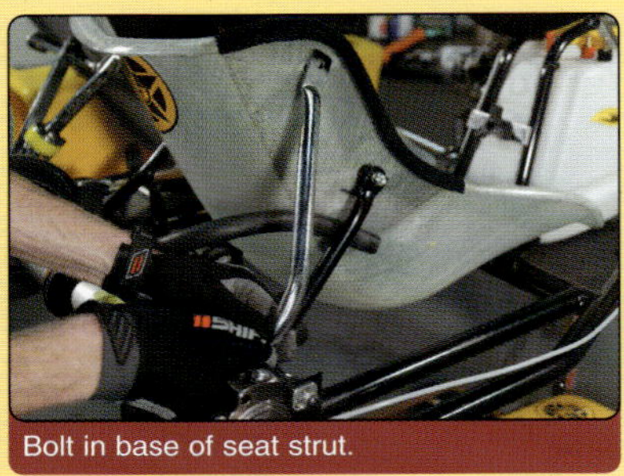
Bolt in base of seat strut.

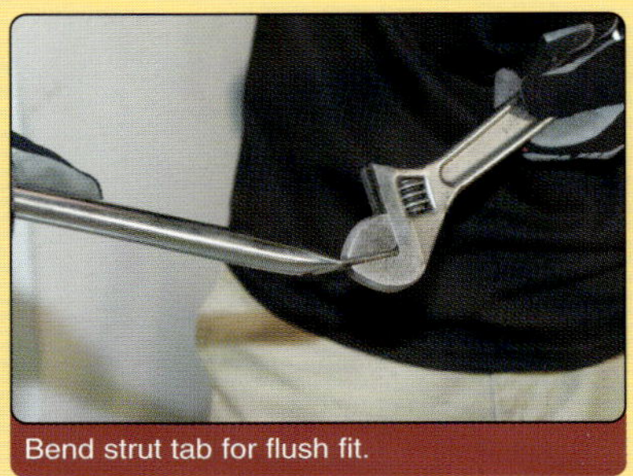
Bend strut tab for flush fit.

Base Line

In this section we are going to help you understand handling characteristics that will give you an idea of a properly set up seat.

Seat Height

With respect to handling, I like to think of the kart as a triangle with the intersection points being the driver's head and the two rear wheels as seen from behind. The steeper the sides of the triangle, the more weight transfer will occur in your kart. In order to achieve the same amount of weight transfer in a kart, the shorter driver will have to have a seat that is mounted considerably higher than the taller driver. Think of the triangle measurement. On a shorter driver, the vertical lines drawn from the rear tires to his head will be considerably less steep than the same lines drawn through the taller driver's head. Some set-ups or track conditions favor shorter drivers, while others may favor taller drivers. Let's look at both cases.

On a track with a lot of grip, the kart will tend to pick up the inside rear wheel much easier without the help of a lot of weight jacking or weight transfer from the driver. So, a taller driver may be continually trying to do things to the kart to settle it down, in other words keep the inside rear tire from picking up too much and hopping. Because of the taller driver's height, lowering the seat to lower the weight transfer can only be done to a certain point before grinding off the bottom of the seat on the track. The shorter guy, on the other hand, has the ability to get much lower in the kart and has an advantage in that area of set-up.

However, on a track that has very little grip the taller driver may have an advantage. On a track that has little grip the kart has a hard time developing enough weight transfer to pick up the inside rear tire and keep the kart from under steering. So, the shorter driver is now faced with a kart that lays so flat on the track he has a serious push. The shorter driver will then be continually trying to raise the mounting of the seat to get the same weight transfer as the taller driver. On very slick tracks, the shorter driver may simply not weigh enough to lift the inside rear wheel.

Seat Angle

Seat angle has a similar effect to seat height. Generally, the steeper the angle, the higher the driver's head, the more weight transfer will happen. I have found that the area of the corner that angle has the biggest effect is mid-corner. Remember, in order to keep the kart from under steering, you must keep the inside rear tire from laying flat on the ground. This also applies in the middle of the corner. For this reason, I always tend to run a fairly steep seat angle and will make other adjustments to keep the kart from hopping.

A sign of a seat that is mounted with too much forward angle is excessive hopping. Too much forward angle also causes the front end to dart, making the kart hard to drive. If your seat is too reclined, your kart will have a tendency to under steer by laying too flat on the ground, making the kart unresponsive with a delayed response when you turn.

Tire Compound

There is a consistent rule when you are relating tire compound to seat position. That is, the harder the tire compound, the less weight transfer you will achieve from the tire. With a softer compound, the more weight transfer you will get. By now this should make pretty good sense. For harder tire classes you will tend to have seats mounted higher and with more seat angle. The opposite will be true with softer tires.

The adjustment of the seat from front to back reacts different with every kart. This means that after you set the seat position to the factory baseline specifications, you need to try to move the seat and see what happens. I will usually go one inch at a time on a new kart just to get an idea of how the change will affect the kart's handling.

Some people think that whenever you move the seat forward you get more front grip, and when you move the seat backward you get more rear grip. This is just not the case. Yes, it may happen that more grip is gained on the front by moving the seat forward. However, it may just as easily be that with more weight on the front end, the front of the kart reacts slower and you actually get more understeer.

Likewise, moving the seat back and loading the rear tires with more weight may give you more rear grip. However, moving the seat back may create a pendulum effect where the rear tires just cannot maintain grip with all your weight moving around and they actually loose grip. So, the bottom line is bring a cordless drill to the track and be prepared to make some changes to hopefully find out what works for you and your particular kart.

Engine Configuration

Engine style will also change where you will need to position your seat. On an engine that sits high in the frame, you will want to mount the seat lower than with an engine that sits low in the frame. This really only applies to the differences from an ICC-style to a moto style engine. An ICC style engine is much shorter and has less effect on weight transfer than its moto counterpart. So, if you happen to switch back and forth between the two, a moto engine should require a slightly lower seat than the same kart with an ICC, to keep the weight transfer similar.

Keeping your seat in shape

The best thing you can do for your seat is to keep all the hardware tight. This will stop the seat from moving and rounding out the holes. The other thing that can make a seat last considerably longer is to always make sure that the mounting surfaces are parallel and that the seat does not make those cracking sounds when you tighten the bolts.

I like to take my seat out after every other day of driving the kart. This gives me a good chance to visually inspect and clean it, along with checking for chaffing or wear on other areas of the kart like hoses and fuel lines. With the seat out, use a contact style cleaner to remove all the grease and grime followed by Simple Green cleaner to get rid of the rest of the dirt or stains.

If you went too low with your seat and ground out the bottom, remember that a kart seat can be repaired with fiberglass. That also applies to the sides of the seat if you happen to crack or wear out the holes. However, keep in mind that a heavily repaired seat will react stiffer and may slightly change the handling of your kart.

Seat should be level with frame.

Make sure the washers mount flush.

cool trick

For fully padded seats draw a circle on the bottom of the seat around the spacers. Then use a spare spacer to mark the center hole to be drilled.

Measuring distance from top of axle.

ENGINE SET-UP

Yamaha YZ 85 moto engine.

Swedetech 125cc Honda moto engine.

TM 125cc ICC Engine.

The need for speed

Just the sound of a shifter kart is enough to move you. The first time you run through the gears is an experience you will never forget. It really is a unique driving sensation. Learning to work the engine to its full potential is a big step for most drivers who are new to shifter karting. Having horsepower, gears and a clutch at your disposal can be a real challenge. It is the engine itself, which is the heart and soul of a shifter kart that distinguishes it from other karts. The evolution of the shifter kart was an obvious next step for karting drivers searching for more speed and performance.

Shifter kart engines have evolved on two parallel paths. In North America much attention has been put on the moto style engine while in Europe much of the work has been on purpose-built engines called Intercontinental C or ICC. Each engine format has unique features and benefits.

The moto engine is exactly as the name implies. These engines were designed and built for off-road motorcycles. The major motorcycle companies like Honda, Yamaha, Kawasaki, Suzuki and TM build these engines. Many adaptations had to be developed to get these engines to work properly on a kart. First, a special type of engine mount needed to be developed to accommodate the mounting positions that are used on a kart.

Next was the pipe. Because of the differences in power requirements and mounting limitations, the pipe for a bike is much different than what is required for a kart. Motocross bikes also use a wet clutch because they are designed to take the abuse of a riding technique that has the rider constantly slipping the clutch.

An ICC engine, on the other hand, is purpose-built to work only on karts. For that reason the fit and finish look much nicer and less bulky on a kart than its moto engine counterpart. The major differences are that on an ICC engine, the exhaust pipe exits to the rear and the intake is located on the front of the engine. Many, but not all the engines, come standard with a dry clutch due to the fact that a shifter kart only uses the clutch to exit the pits and start the race. Usually, at no other time will you slip the clutch.

Two Stroke Basics

The two-stroke engine is truly an amazing engineering marvel because it can produce tremendous horsepower given its compact and simple design. Carburetion and exhaust are key components that need to work together in order to maximize the engine's potential. We will look not only at how a two-stroke creates power, but also three key principles that will dictate how much power is delivered. These are engine temperature, power band and air density.

Basically, a two stroke operates by compressing a mixture of fuel and air in the cylinder and the crankcase. The fuel is itself a mixture of gasoline and oil, premixed to required specifications. The fuel/air mixture moves through the engine by making use of the vacuum and pressure created by the piston moving up and down.

The use of the term two-stroke comes from the fact that the engine performs all the functions in two strokes of the piston, and the spark plug fires every time the piston reaches top dead center. A two-stroke engine accomplishes in 360° what a four-stroke engine takes 720° to complete. For example, during the downward path of the piston, known as the power stroke, the fuel/air mixture in the crankcase is compressed and forced through the transfer ports up into the combustion chamber, which pushes the spent fuel out the exhaust port.

So what stops the new fuel/air mix from escaping out the exhaust port? Any waste gasses that hang around after combustion are used to plug the exhaust port for the next intake stroke. This occurs as the shockwave created from the combustion travels into the exhaust pipe.

The engines we will look at here are reed valve style. Reed valves are used to control the flow of the fuel/air mixture into the engine. The reed valve is a flap that opens when crankcase pressure is below atmospheric pressure and closes when crankcase pressure is above atmospheric pressure. The reeds are made of fiberglass or carbon fibre.

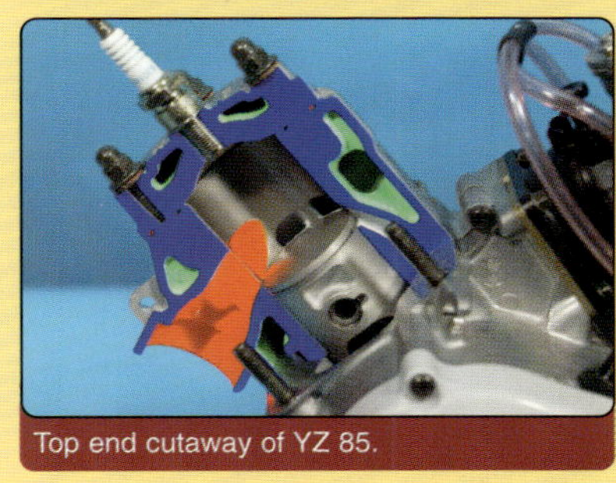
Top end cutaway of YZ 85.

Engine Temperature

Two stroke engines can generate a great deal of heat, especially at the key touching points. The most notable of these is the piston skirt and the cylinder barrel. When a two-stroke engine overheats, seizure of the piston skirt and the cylinder wall will occur. They literally weld together for an instant and stop the engine from turning.

Another area susceptible to overheating is the combustion chamber itself. Running a lean fuel/air mixture will cause intense heat at the point of combustion, when the piston is at top dead center. The result is that the piston crown will actually begin to melt, which in turn will rob the engine of power and lead to seizure.

The liquid cooling of engines has helped to increase horsepower by increasing the usable RPM range and keeping temperatures in an acceptable range. The added weight from a cooling system is more than made up for in increased power and longer engine life.

Transfer ports are marked in white.

Power Band

All two-stroke engines have a power band. This is the range of RPM in which the maximum power output is achieved. This power band can be moved up and down the RPM range to work with the conditions at hand. Basically, a two-stroke is a very high revving engine. Moto engines run as high as 13,000 RPM, while ICC engines can run over 14,000 RPM. The majority of the power tends to be concentrated in a range of about 1,200 to 1,500 RPM in duration and usually does not appear until about 11,000 RPM.

Exhaust ports are marked in orange.

The power band is basically the perfect match of the expansion chamber shockwave and the combustion stroke. It can feel like an extra kick of power from the engine. When the engine is outside the power band, the RPM range is too low or too high for the combustion stroke and the shockwave to have the proper timing.

The volume of the expansion chamber and the length of the pipe dictate the timing of the shockwave. Therefore, we can tune the exhaust port and the expansion chamber to put the power band where it will work best given the conditions we are facing.

Cooling area is marked in green.

Air Density

Air density, or the relative weight of the air, is the combination of three different elements: barometric pressure, air temperature and water

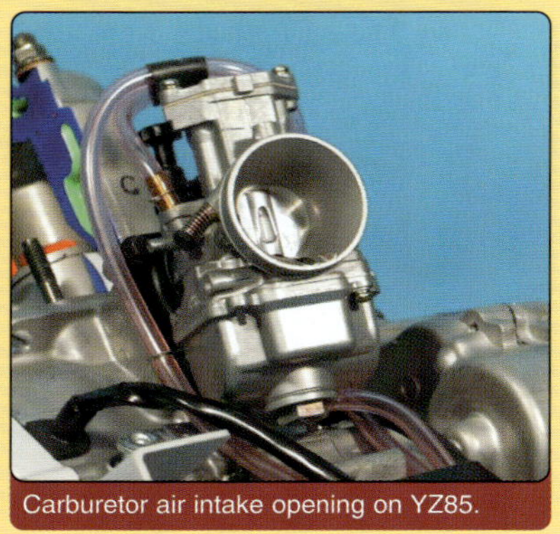
Carburetor air intake opening on YZ85.

vapor. The air's density is generally highest at sea level because the barometric pressure is high and the temperature is low. A good example is a cold and sunny winter day. On the other hand, air density will be lowest at a high elevation where the barometric pressure is generally low and the temperature is high. The amount of water vapor is measured by humidity, which is the least significant factor when evaluating air density. The only true way to measure air density is with an air density gauge.

Why is air density important? With each stroke of the engine the exact same volume of air is drawn, but the density or weight of that volume of air can vary greatly from day to day and even hour by hour. For example, at high elevations our engines are getting less air, so the engine needs less fuel to maintain the desired fuel/air mixture. So, if the density increases and we do not increase the amount of fuel, the mixture will be lean, which can lead to a siezed piston. Conversely, if the density decreases and we do not reduce the fuel volume, the mixture will be rich and the engine will be robbed of horsepower.

Remember, something else goes down as altitude goes up: horsepower. You can expect to lose as much as 3% of your power for every 1,000 feet (304.8 metres) that you rise in altitude. So, what does all of this mean? Cold air is dense air and dense air requires bigger jets. Warm air is thin air and thin air requires smaller jets. Air temperature makes that much of a difference. Always take constant readings of air density and note other weather conditions such as temperature, clouds, proximity to water and other meteorological factors.

Swedetech 125cc cylinder.

Key Components

Most shifter kart drivers have a good idea of the basic components that make up a two-stroke engine. The part that throws some drivers for a loop is the crankcase and transmission. It can be confusing to understand that they are two separate components linked by a gear on the crankshaft. The pre-mixed fuel/air mixture that flows through to the transfer ports lubricates the crankcase including the connecting rod and main bearings. The transmission is located in a separate area and uses different oil for lubricating the gears.

Cylinder

The cylinder, sometimes called the barrel, is made of a light alloy and has a very durable steel sleeve or plating called nikelsel. The cylinder has transfer ports cast into it, which allow the fuel/air mixture to flow from the carburetor, through the crankcase, to the combustion chamber.

Polished cylinder head.

Cylinder Head

The cylinder head sits on top of the cylinder and accommodates the spark plug. The shape of the cylinder head helps to determine the volume of the combustion chamber. Because the cylinder head is subject to so much heat, it is also a major area for cooling. The cylinder head will also have an outlet that leads hot water back to the radiator for cooling.

Piston

The piston is made of light alloy, with a single ring at the top that runs along the cylinder walls to seal in compression. It is the top of the piston, the cylinder head and the cylinder barrel that combine to create the combustion chamber.

Connecting Rod

The connecting rod is generally made from forged steel. It needs to be extremely strong to take the shock of the combustion and transfer that energy to the crankshaft. A needle bearing is used at the top of the rod to connect to the piston wrist pin. A needle bearing is used to connect the bottom of the rod to the crankshaft.

Piston, pin, bearing and clip.

Transmission

The transmission of a shifter kart is what really brings the package to life. It is described as a synchro-mesh design, which allows the gears to be selected in sequential order. There is a slight gap between first and second gear for neutral, which is basically a spot where no gear exists. This is an extremely compact transmission that allows for very rapid gear selection with minimal input. The only down side is that you must go through each gear. You cannot jump from fifth down to second in one movement.

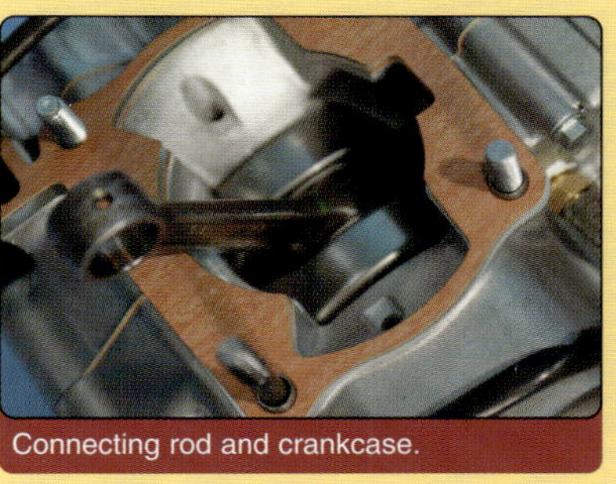
Connecting rod and crankcase.

Clutch

As we discussed earlier, shifter karts use two different types of clutches. Whether a wet style clutch, or a dry clutch, they function the same way. The clutch is made up of two types of interleafing plates, called friction and drive plates. The main drive gear turns one set of plates, while the other set of plates drive the transmission gear. The plates are all gathered in a basket one in between the other, pulled together by a set of springs.

Friction forces the drive plates to turn the transmission plates. Pull the clutch lever and the plates move apart, taking the friction away, allowing the kart to run in gear, while at a stand still. The wet style clutch uses the oil to keep the plates cool and widen the friction range. The release of a dry clutch is more like a switch, on or off.

hot tip

When selecting gears when the engine is not running, try to move the rear wheels back and forth. This will make finding the gear much easier and save wear on the transmission gears and shift forks.

Ignition

The ignition of a two stroke delivers the spark that starts the combustion. The initial electrical charge comes from a magneto that runs off the crankshaft. A two stroke does not require a battery to operate and can produce enough of its own electrical charge to run on.

The initial electrical pulse goes into an ignition box or CDI (constant discharge ignition). The ignition box meters and co-ordinates the delivery of the pulse. From the ignition box, the charge goes to the coil, which amplifies the charge to the voltage level required to ignite the fuel/air mixture. From the coil an electrical charge is sent to the spark plug.

Base Line Tuning

When tuning a two-stroke engine, always think of the engine as the total measure from the main jet in the carburetor, to the end of the exhaust pipe. Adjusting anything within this range by size or length will in fact alter the performance of the engine. The main tell-tale is the spark plug and the top of the piston. This is the critical point of combustion, where all the elements come together in a split second to create the maximum horsepower.

To better understand how to tune your engine, we will look at spark plug reading, ignition timing, carburetor jetting and pipe tuning. The

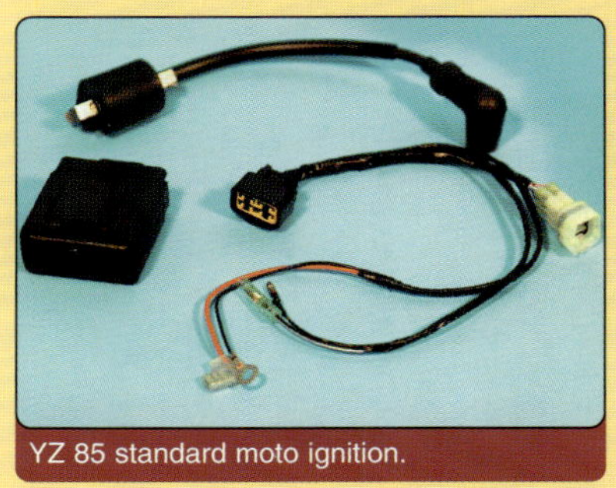
YZ 85 standard moto ignition.

hot tip

Never try to read an old plug. A new plug will give a clearer idea as to what is happening inside your engine.

Spark plug running properly.

Signs the engine running lean.

Signs the engine is running rich.

order of this list is very important. In order to maximize your tuning efforts, you need to progress in a systematic manner.

Spark Plug Reading

One of the key elements of a spark plug is a property called heat range. All conventional plugs have to stay hot enough to burn away deposits such as oil and carbon that could build up on the electrodes. This build up would have the effect of short-circuiting or "fouling" the plug. To be safe, plug temperatures should be between 700° F (371° C) and 1,000° F (537.8° C) over the whole range of operating conditions.

It is important to understand that it is the engine that puts heat into the plug and not the reverse. Therefore, a "hot" plug does not make an engine run hotter and neither does a "cold" plug make the engine run cooler. Knowing which plugs are hotter or colder than the ones you presently have in your engine is easy if you stay with the same brand. Nearly all of the plug manufacturers use a numbering system to designate the heat range. This information is readily available on their websites.

So how can you tell if you are running the correct heat range? Always ask your engine builder. The spark plug will get hot enough to keep the insulator nose completely clean, with all deposit burned away, but not so hot that the electrodes show signs of overheating. The primary evidence that a plug is overheating can be found on the plug's center electrode. The edges on the tip of the electrode will show signs of being rounded by erosion or melting. Try to use a new plug that has been subjected to only a few minutes of running.

Most of us know detonation as the piston killer. The spark plug can tell you when and why detonation is occurring in your engine. The spark plug can also tell you just how much spark advance and what jetting your engine needs. Basically, firing the spark plug too early will produce detonation as the mixture out in the chamber's far corners gets enough time to reach explosion-level temperature. Also, a slightly lean fuel/air mixture detonates at a lower temperature. So, it's all a matter of ignition timing and fuel/air mixture.

The best reading of a spark plug comes from a "plug chop" meaning the engine should be cut on "full song" to accurately read the color of the fuel/air mixture. As we talked about in the first chapter, your engine will have no idle setting, so when you let off the gas the engine will stall. To do a plug chop, come in off the track fast without a cool down lap and immediately cut the engine and let it stall. Then you can remove the spark plug and read exactly what occurred in the combustion chamber at high RPM.

Ignition Timing

Now that you can read what the engine is doing by looking at the plug and piston, you need to dial in your ignition timing. The purpose of ignition timing is to maximize the power created by combustion. An advanced timing causes the spark to happen before top dead center (TDC), which is great for low to mid RPM because the mixture has more time to burn and create more pressure in the combustion chamber. The down side is that more heat is created. The impact of more heat is even greater as the RPM rises.

So, we want to fire the plug closer to TDC as the RPM rises. The closer the plug fires to TDC the less pressure rise and the less heat. The overall advantage is that the more heat is put into the pipe and less into the combustion chamber. This has the effect of increasing the RPM range and reducing the possibility of melt down.

It is important to stress that you need to give spark advance very close attention because excessive spark lead is the most frequent cause of detonation. When the spark is advanced too much the pressure rise in the combustion chamber is too great and creates a ping sound. This is a major warning that you have gone too far and a seizure is imminent.

The timing of the spark can be controlled in the CDI and at the magneto. On the side of the magneto is a stator plate, which can be moved forward or backward to advance or retard the timing of the electrical pulse. This is usually measured in degrees. The problem is that when you advance the timing at the magneto, you change it for the entire RPM range.

The CDI has a built-in curve, which alters the spark timing over the RPM range allowing for peak power. A programmable ignition, found on moto style engines, allows you to not only create your own curve, but also a number of different curves that you can switch to as you drive. The driver can then select the one that works best for him in different situations, at different tracks or stages of a race.

Carburetor Jetting

With ignition timing now under control, you can further fine-tune your engine with jetting. Jetting is a constant adjustment because of changing air density. In this section we will look at the four different adjustments, how they work together to create a 'circuit' and what part of the RPM range they affect.

The airscrew is located on the side of the carburetor and affects jetting for initial throttle response. If your throttle response is abrupt (like an on/off switch) your airscrew may be set too rich. If your throttle response is too soft you may try to richen the airscrew. By turning the screw out, (counter clockwise) you will make the mixture leaner, while turning the air screw in will make the mixture richer.

The slide is like a door that moves up and down in the carburetor. The slide has a cutout on the front, which also affects throttle response. Because the cutout is on the air box side of the carburetor it will affect the amount of initial air that is allowed to mix with the fuel. The bigger the cutout, the more air will mix and the leaner the mixture will be. Just like the airscrew, the size of the slide will make a big change to the drivability when you first crack open the throttle. If response is too abrupt, try a slide with a bigger cutout. Generally, for maximum torque, you want as rich a fuel/air mixture as possible (a smaller cutout), without sacrificing drivability.

The pilot jet controls the low-speed and idle mixture. It will come into play just after the airscrew. On the track, the pilot jet affects initial throttle response, but has most of its effect just as the RPMs start to build. The pilot jets are stamped with numbers that let you know what size they are. Generally speaking, for maximum torque, you want to run as rich a pilot as possible. Getting either too rich or too lean will show with drivability problems similar to the airscrew.

The needle jet and emulsion tube combine to control the amount of fuel mixing with the air at low to mid-range throttle. The needle is

warning

If you mistakenly drop your spark plug on the ground, never re-use it and put it back in the engine. The porcelain in the center of the spark plug can easily become cracked and if re-used may fall into your engine causing damage.

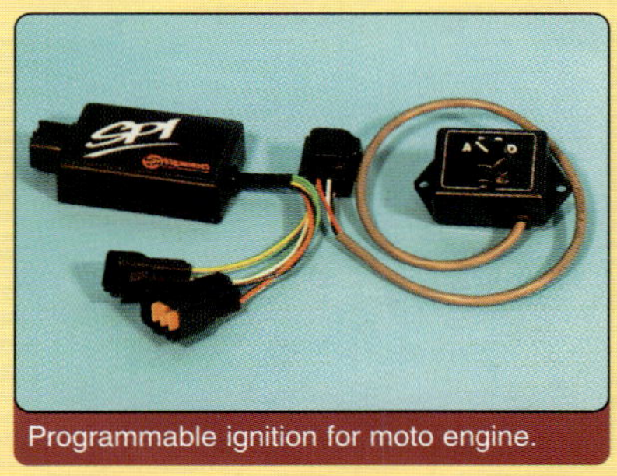

Programmable ignition for moto engine.

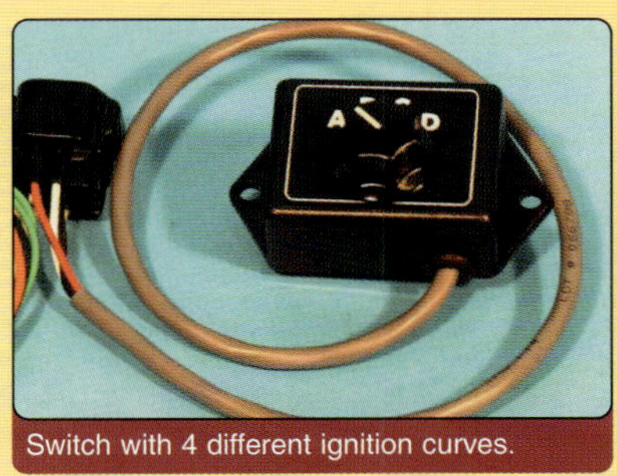

Switch with 4 different ignition curves.

hot tip

When doing a plug chop and coasting into the pits, it is important that you take care in downshifting the gearbox when the engine is not running. Damage will result if you don't let your speed drop before you start to go down through the gears. Although the engine may be at 0 RPM, the kart is coasting at 30mph (55.6kmp), which means the gears are spinning at a fast rate.

indirectly connected to the throttle cable by way of the slide, while the emulsion tube is attached at the bottom of the carburetor. When you open the throttle, the needle lifts out of the emulsion tube. The fuel passes through the emulsion tube and into the intake manifold. The bigger the inside of the emulsion tube, the more fuel that can pass between it and the needle, creating a richer mixture.

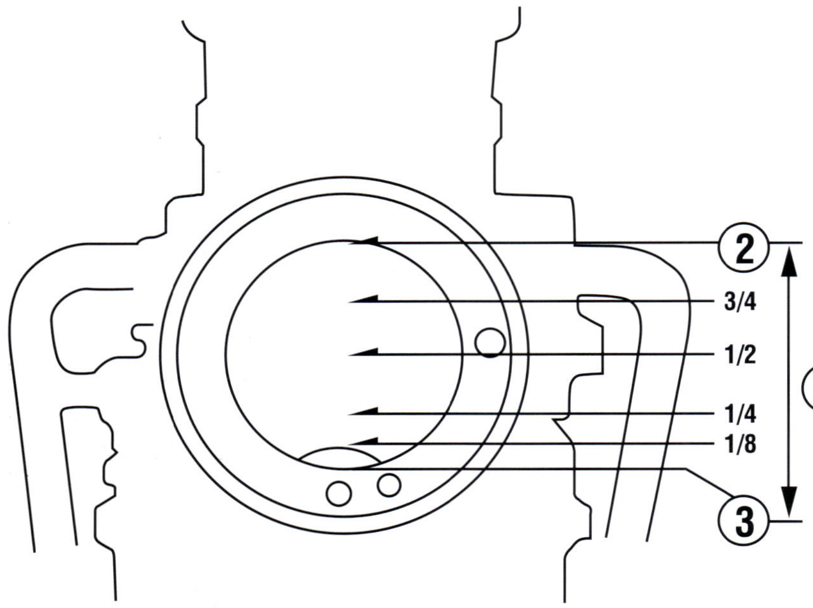

Reprinted courtesy of Yamaha Motor Company Ltd.

Conversely, a smaller diameter needle would allow more fuel to pass between it and the tube, again creating a richer mixture. So to lean the fuel/air mixture, either use a smaller emulsion tube or a thicker needle. The emulsion tube has a number stamped on its side that designates the size of the inside of the tube. Just like the emulsion tube, the needle is also marked to say what size and taper it is. Along with actually changing the needle or the emulsion tube to get the desired mixture, there are usually five slots that are used to make adjustments. By adjusting the C-clip up or down, you can change the position or height of the needle in the tube, which will vary the mixture. The higher the needle or lower the clip, the richer the mixture will be and vice versa.

The main jet comes into play from mid-throttle to full throttle. The bigger the main jet, the richer the engine will run. The main jet controls the mixture at full throttle applications and consequently has a big effect on straightaway speed and lap time. It is very important to get the main jet mixture correct not only for power, but also for wear and/or possible seizure of your engine. As with most of the possible adjustments with your carburetor, too rich a mixture will not make the optimum power.

Because of the area of high RPM that the main jet controls, too lean a mixture could have a catastrophic result. Being too lean will make the piston run hotter which means more expansion and a tighter piston to cylinder clearance. Also, too lean will starve the cylinder wall and the lower connecting rod bearing of the oil that is in the fuel mixture. It's not that you should never try to fine-tune your main jet size, it's just very important to adjust in small steps and try to have the help of someone that has the experience to recognize when the main jet is too lean.

As with any jetting changes, in order to get an accurate picture you need to do a "plug chop" when coming into the pits. As we discussed before, this means exiting the track without a cool down lap and immediately letting the engine come to a stop, coasting into the pits with the clutch engaged.

You will find that all the different types of jets overlap. For example, when the airscrew stops having an effect, the pilot jet starts controlling the mixture. As in any circuit in the carburetor, as one starts to taper off, the next circuit or jet will start to come into effect. Always start rich and then work your way toward lean. Keep changes small and deliberate. Keep an eye on the air density. Never try to jet too close to the perfect mixture until you have taken care of spark advance. The fuel/air mixture that will yield the most power is only slightly richer than the mixture that can cause detonation.

Setting part		Throttle valve opeing
		Full-closed 1/4 1/2 3/4 Full-open
Pilot jet Pilot air screw		
Jet needle	Diameter of straight portion	
	Clip position	
Main jet		

① Throttle valve opening
② Full-open
③ Full-closed

Reprinted courtesy of Yamaha Motor Company Ltd.

You can use the combustion chamber and piston to tell you when there is even slight detonation inside the engine. Look at the top of the piston through the spark plug hole with a bend-a-light to see how the engine is running. Signs of detonation will show as tiny pits on the top of the piston. The piston crown will show detonation sooner than the spark plug will. If the piston is detonating toward the exhaust side, the main jet is too lean. If the piston is detonating toward the intake side, the pilot jet and the needle are too lean.

When using a typical moto engine carburetor like a Kehien or Mikuni, start working with the main jet, and then the pilot jet. Then, if necessary, work with the needle. However, on an ICC engine using a Delorto carburetor, work with the main jet first and stay close behind with the emulsion tube and needle. Then, if necessary, work with the pilot jet to set your tuning.

Pipe Tuning

The next area to look at is pipe tuning. This tends to be more track specific and not atmospheric like carburetor tuning. The question is whether the track is fast with long sweepers or short with hard hairpins. The exhaust pipe or expansion chamber for a two stroke is made up of five specific parts. The part connecting to the cylinder is the head, followed by the diffuser cone. The next section is called the dwell followed by the baffle cone and finally the stinger. The length and angle of each of

RLV pipe for YZ 85.

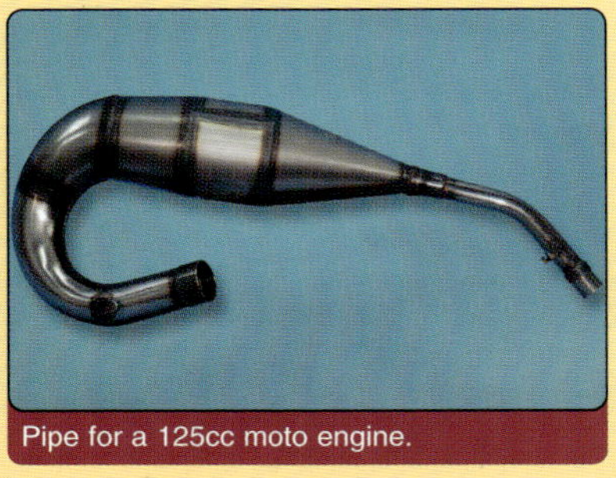
Pipe for a 125cc moto engine.

Pipe for TM 125cc ICC engine.

ICC, 125cc moto and 80cc moto silencer.

these sections can be adjusted to affect the overall engine performance. Remember, the pipe needs to be tuned in order to match the flow of exhaust gases from the exhaust port to the return shockwave in the pipe. In general, the volume of a pipe is 12 times larger than the cylinder volume. Because shifter karts need to have the horsepower made at very high RPM the header length is quite short.

The pipe on a two stroke is truly a magical thing. It has a huge impact on the performance of the engine by harnessing the shockwave or pressure pulse created in the combustion chamber. As this wave travels down the pipe, it moves at the speed of sound and remains unchanged until it enters the diffuser cone.

As the diameter of the pipe increases, it reflects a negative wave back toward the engine. The original wave continues down the pipe and enters the baffle or reverse diffuser. At this point the wave is reflected back toward the engine as a positive pressure wave. This is the magic of a two stroke. The negative wave sucks the remaining exhaust gasses out of the cylinder on the power stroke. The positive wave stops the new fuel/air mixture from escaping the cylinder in the combustion stroke.

The length of the pipe and the temperature inside the pipe will control the timing of these waves. So, a longer pipe means a lower power band which is good for short, tight tracks. A shorter pipe means a higher power band, which is good for faster longer tracks.

Pipe design is very complicated and changing any part of the pipe will most likely result in poor performance at best and engine seizure at worst. The only time some one should alter the pipe is if you cannot find a gear ratio that fits the track. The length of the pipe header can be adjusted by putting spacers between the exhaust port and the pipe that would allow you to run a taller ratio.

Top End Rebuild

In this section we will go over a quick piston and ring change for your engine. Changing the ring regularly is good engine maintenance. The cylinder, cylinder head and possibly the connecting rod will need attention at some point. This is where your engine builder can be your best source for coaching and advice on engine maintenance. Use the engine log on page 3 in the appendix to keep a detailed log of your engine program. This will prove very valuable as you learn to tune your engine and run through regular engine maintenance.

Start by removing all the water from the cooling system. You may need to tip the kart to make sure all the water is out. Remove the water hose from the top of the cylinder head. Remove the exhaust pipe completely. Remove the carburetor and the air breather.

Pull off the plug cap and remove the spark plug. Put the plug back in the box and look at it later. Loosen the nuts on the head and at the base of the cylinder. Remove the head and place it on the bench with the top down. Lift the cylinder slowly from the crankcase. Make sure you have a clean rag to place the cylinder on. When the cylinder is removed, place a clean rag around the connecting rod to protect the crankcase from any debris. Remove the old ring very carefully. Make sure you do not scratch the piston.

Place the new ring in the cylinder to check the gap. If the gap measures less than 8/1,000 of an inch on an 80cc engine or 10/1,000 on a 125cc engine, use a file to open the gap. If the gap measures more than 20/1000 of an inch, try another ring.

Remove the old base gasket and the top gaskets or O-rings. Make sure the mounting surface is clean of any debris. Put on the new gaskets and O-rings. These gaskets do not require any gasket sealer of any kind.

Remove one of the C-clips from the side of the piston. You can see a small indent that exposes part of the clip. Use a round dull scribe to pop the clip out. Immediately throw the clip into the trash so you do not accidentally use it again. Push the pin out from the opposite side with your finger, until it clears the bearing. Lift the piston off and push the pin all the way through. Remove the other C-clip and throw it into the trash along with the pin. If the piston is in good shape, keep it for an emergency.

As you assemble the top end put a couple of drops of pre-mix on each part before you put them together. Put the new ring on to the new piston very carefully. Put one C-clip into the piston and start the new pin into the piston on the opposite side. Place the piston over the rod, align the new bearing and push the pin through very carefully. Once the pin is fully in place, put the other C-clip into the piston.

Before we put the cylinder back on it should be cleaned and inspected. Check the cylinder walls for wear. Use WD40 and a green Scotch Brite pad to clean the cylinder bore. Clean in a cross pattern similar to the original pattern on the cylinder wall. Finally, wash the cylinder with soap and water and dry immediately. Coat the cylinder walls with pre-mix. Now we can slide the cylinder back on. The base of the cylinder is slightly beveled. Squeeze the ring with one hand and slide on the cylinder. Once in place put the nuts on finger tight

Now inspect the head and polish it with an aluminum-polishing agent. Tighten the bolts on the cylinder in a cross pattern starting with the right front. Put on the head and tighten in a cross pattern. Refer to your owner's manual or check with your engine builder for the correct torque settings. Replace all the components.

Basic Engine Break-in

If your engine is brand new or has a new top end you need to do a basic engine break-in. It is recommended that you start with a larger or richer jet. Ask your engine builder what the proper jet size is for engine break-in.

With the engine fired, place your hand on the cylinder and feel the engine come up to temperature. This should take between five and ten minutes. While the engine is running always vary the RPM at the low end of the RPM range. Stop the engine and allow it to cool down. With the engine now cooled down, strap on your gear and head out on the track.

Gently roll into the throttle as you exit the corners and roll out of the throttle before you get the RPM too high. Prolonged high RPM will kill an engine on break-in. Keep shifts short to keep RPMs at the mid range. It is important that you vary your RPMs on the track in order to seat the ring properly. This session should last about 10 minutes.

For a brand new engine or a complete rebuild, it is usually a good idea to double the break in time, adding a little more RPM as you go. Change the jet back to the original size as indicated by your engine builder and put in a fresh plug. If the break-in was for a new engine, it is

Loosen the nuts on the head.

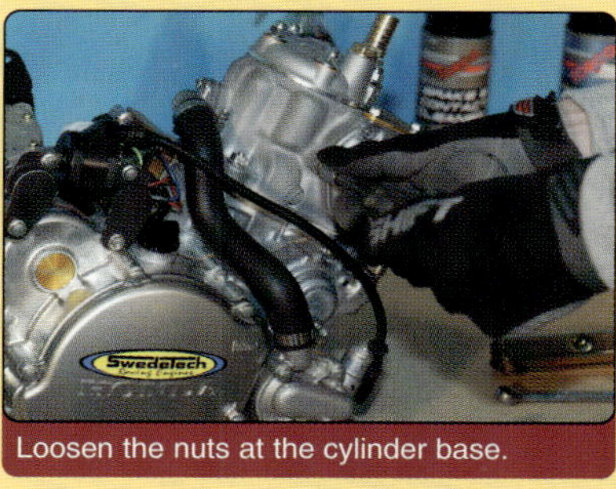

Loosen the nuts at the cylinder base.

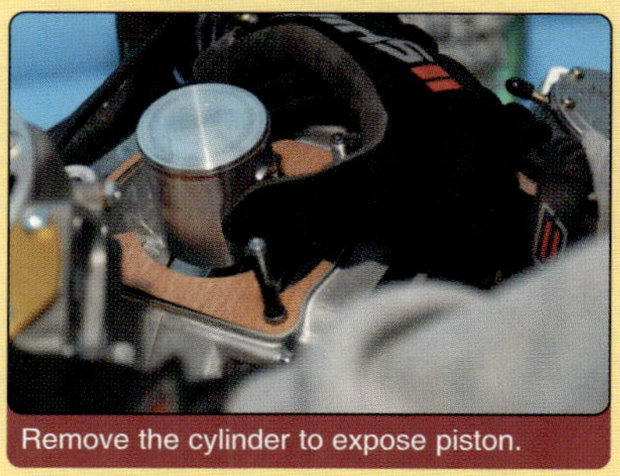
Remove the cylinder to expose piston.

Put a clean rag over the crankcase.

Pull out the pin carefully.

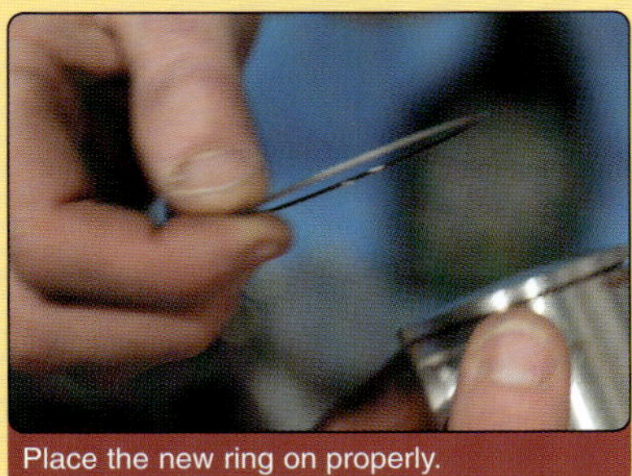
Place the new ring on properly.

Be careful not to scratch the piston.

Line up the pin with the groove.

Coat the bearing with some pre-mix.

a good idea to change transmission oil to remove any contamination caused by gear wear-in. Check for leaks around the cylinder, carburetor and pipe.

Storage

If your engine is to be stored for 60 days or more, some preventive measures must be taken to avoid deterioration. After cleaning off all the grease, grit and grime, you need to prepare the engine for long-term storage.

First, drain the fuel tank, fuel lines and the carburetor float bowl, just like we do after each race day. This time pull the carburetor off and spray it with carburetor cleaner. Move the slide up and down making sure the carburetor is free of any fuel. Put the carburetor back on and place a rag in the end.

Remove the entire exhaust system. Wipe the pipe and silencer down thoroughly and apply a generous coating of WD40 to keep any surfaces from rusting. Place in a large plastic bag and place in your seat. Put a clean rag in the exhaust port.

Next, remove the spark plug and spray a little WD40 into the combustion chamber. With the plug in the plug cap and properly grounded, put the kart in gear and turn the rear wheels. This will coat the cylinder walls with a protective coating. Put the spark plug back in.

Next you need to think about draining the water out of the cooling system. This is only necessary if the temperature in your area will fall below freezing, otherwise leave the water in and top it up as required. To drain the system start by loosening the hose clamp at the water pump. For moto engines this is on the engine at the front. Loosen the radiator cap and tilt the kart to the right. For ICC style engines the pump is at the back of the kart. Tilt the kart backward to make sure all the water runs out.

hot tip

When inserting the C-clip back into the piston, make sure that the C-clip opening is not located at the notch of the pin opening. The clip could vibrate and pop out of its groove.

hot tip

If you have to break-in an engine on a crowded track, try to stay off line and out of the way.

warning

Never mix two types of oil in the same batch; clotting of the oil could result. Be sure to drain the fuel tank and the carburetor float bowl of old premix prior to filling with the new premix.

DATA ACQUISITION SET-UP

Keeping an eye on your data.

It is all in the numbers

As the name of this chapter implies, data acquisition is the collection of information and the process of converting that information to see if changes have made you faster or slower. Data acquisition is a gauge of your progress throughout the day. The hardest and most critical part of having data acquisition is reading it properly. I like to think of data acquisition systems as a fancy and expensive notebook. They are not some magic Genie that will tell you how to go faster. You need to be very careful not to let data acquisition steer you in the wrong direction, by misreading the numbers.

Although not cheap to purchase, a data acquisition system is a good investment. When used properly, data acquisition is something that will help you gain that extra tenth of a second. Regardless of what system you purchase, always consult the manufacturer for correct mounting, use and care of your system. The manufacturer is your best source of information to ensure you get the most from your data acquisition unit.

Our first goal is to gain an understanding of all of the key readings that data acquisition can draw on, in order to understand what we are measuring. The power of data acquisition is having the ability to make changes to your kart based on very specific information, which will back up your "seat of the pants" feeling.

hot tip

In order to get lap times before I owned a data acquisition system, I would tye wrap a stopwatch to the top of my steering wheel. When set up properly, you should be able to hit the button and read the time every lap. Buy a stop watch with large buttons and a large display.

Capturing relevant real time data

There are a number of different sensors, or channels, that can be installed on your kart. Some are required to ensure proper engine performance, while others are more advanced and can be used to evaluate driver performance. There are four main categories of data acquisition sensors that I consider to be important to tuning your kart and helping with your driving performance. These are lap times, water temperature, RPM and MPH.

For a driver to get faster, the critical and most basic part of data acquisition is having accurate lap times and engine temperature readings. Lap times will allow you to gauge your progress, while the engine temperature readings will help you to run trouble-free all day.

Why are consistent and visible lap times so important to becoming a better driver? It's all about training your brain. Every lap, your brain is thinking things like, "that feels good" or "that feels slow." By having lap times, you can train yourself to associate a "good feeling" with a faster lap time. Without accurate real-time feedback, you may feel good, but actually be going slower.

The second key sensor to have on your kart is a temperature sensor. There are two types of temperature sensors you can install: water and head temperature. Water temperature readings can be taken from either the water line returning to the radiator from the cylinder head, or from a fitting installed into the radiator itself. Engine temperature can be taken from the top of the cylinder or from the exhaust pipe. When installing the water or engine temperature sensor, you will only require one of each.

So, why have two temperature sensors on your kart? One reason is that with a shifter kart being liquid cooled; we have the opportunity to understand and compare the operating temperatures of the water and the combustion chamber. Your engine builder will be able to give you the correct operating temperature for your engine.

Keep in mind that a cooler temperature will produce more torque and rev less, while a hotter running engine will lose torque but gain RPM. Even more important, having two temperature sensors enables you to see if your cooling system is circulating water. If the water temperature reads cold and the head temperature reads hot, you will know right away that you have a water circulation problem. If undetected, this circulation problem will cause the engine to overheat and possibly seize.

The dash needs to be centered.

The other two sensors that can really make a difference to the typical club racer are RPM and speed. These two are best described as the "results" channels because they show how you are performing on the track.

RPM is important because we want to operate in the proper range to maximize the kart's power output. Unlike the temperature scenario, a driver can hear and feel the RPM range. As you work to fine-tune your engine, trusting only the "seat of your pants" can lead to problems. The problem is that your gut sense may not be accurate and being off a few hundred RPM can mean a significant difference in lap time. Back in the pits, we can look at all the information on the computer using the software supplied by the data acquisition system manufacturer.

Data acquisition is also suited for engine and gear changes. I use RPM and MPH to back up what I'm feeling in the kart. If I make a gear change and think that it is helping my speed on the straightaway, I will always double check with the information from the data acquisition system to back up my feeling. Again, the data will not tell you what to change on your kart, just if the change you made was good or not.

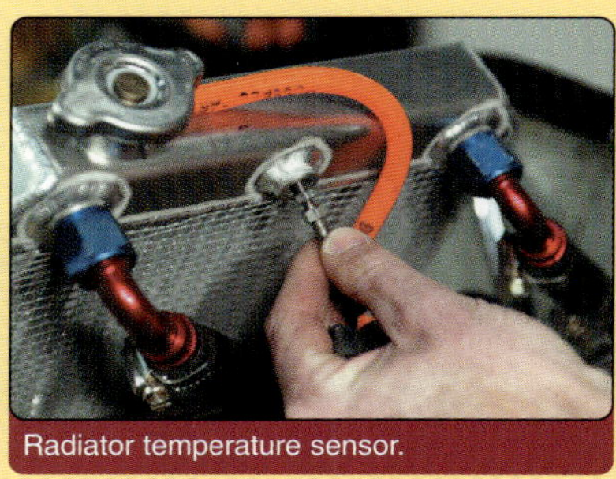

Radiator temperature sensor.

Other benefits of data logging systems, are track mapping capabilities. A driver can look at their laps and understand where the kart is strong and where it can be improved. Remember in chapter two on driving, we talked about being fast in the corner that leads to the longest straight. With data now in front of us, we can in fact determine if this is the case when we make a change in our driving style.

Finally, we can use our system to look at a theoretical fast lap or the perfect lap. With all of our data downloaded into our lap top and loaded in our software, we can take the best of each section and understand what the theoretical best lap could look like. If used consistently, this will help to determine where you can improve your lap time. This is useful on a busy track where it's hard to get a clean lap time with no traffic.

By understanding the engine and chassis configuration, we can understand what the final set-up should look like. For example, if three of the five sections were fastest with the same gear and jetting, while the other two sections were faster with a different jet and gear, there may be a different combination of gear and jet that can yield the best lap time.

With data acquisition installed on the kart, you have increased the workload on driver and crew. While the tuner may be working on the kart, the driver can evaluate the information and begin to formulate a plan. For the recreational driver or club racer, having the data available

Data logging unit with 6 channels.

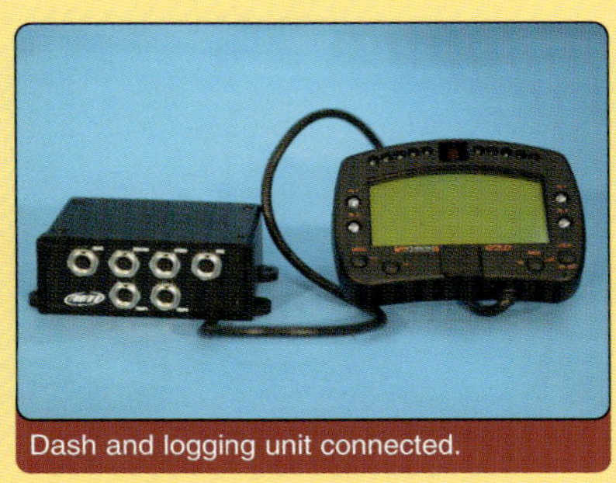
Dash and logging unit connected.

RPM spark plug lead sensor.

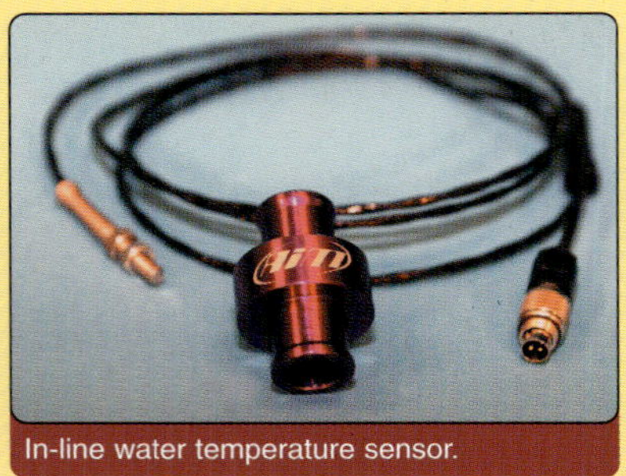
In-line water temperature sensor.

allows you to look at your progress after the race day is complete and begin to think about changes for your next outing.

Key Components

A data acquisition system is actually quite simple to install. You do not have to have a degree in engineering or computer science to make it work. It does take time to learn your specific system and understand how it will work best for you. Make the most of your karting experience and take the time to understand what your system can do for you.

Data Acquisition Unit

The main unit, or brain box, of the system is where all points lead, literally. The main unit connects all of the sensor leads to the software processing and memory storage. Also, it provides the information to the dash for real time presentation or to a laptop for download to special software. The main unit carries the hardware and software that brings the input data to life. Many units, like the MyChron Gold we are installing, can house an accelerometer used to draw out a track map.

Display Dash

The display dash attaches to the steering wheel to give the driver real-time, heads up information on what the sensors are reading. Most systems use numbers and lights to indicate the current status of engine output parameters as well as on-track performance. The main display feature is usually engine operating temperature followed by RPM and then lap time.

Input Pickups

There are a number of sensors that can be installed on your kart. Most systems have at least two channels and some units have as many as six different channels you can monitor.

RPM or engine speed is taken from the spark plug lead. This sensor uses the pulse of spark from the ignition to the spark plug to read the engine RPM. Most sensors clip on top of the spark plug wire in a non-invasive manner.

As we talked about earlier, there are two temperature readings, each of which can be taken from two locations. If only one channel is available, use the engine temperature sensor located at the spark plug. Simply replace the spark plug washer with the sensor ring and tighten down the plug. The other place to read combustion chamber temperature is on the exhaust pipe near the exhaust port. Installation is a little more involved than the plug ring version.

If there are two channels available for temperature monitoring, the second one should be used to monitor the cooling system. The radiator-mounted sensor is easier to install than the inline coupling. Also, the coolant does not need to flow through the coupling, which may reduce the coolant flow.

The MPH or wheel speed can be measured from the front wheel or the rear wheel. Mounting to the front wheel gives you an accurate reading, as no wheel spin will come into play. Some systems recommend mounting on the rear axle, using a collar that has a magnet in it. The magnet passes by the sensor, monitoring the rotation of the axle. When values such as wheel size are added into the system, we get an accurate reading of MPH.

The other sensors that can be installed include one for gear selection, steering input, brake input and throttle input. These sensors are only really valuable if you are comparing the speed or technique from one driver to another.

Beacon

The beacon is a two-part system requiring the beacon itself and a beacon sensor on the kart. The beacon sensor picks up the signal from the trackside. The sensor needs to be mounted with a clear line of site to the beacon. The beacon and the beacon sensor need to be at the same height to ensure an accurate reading.

The beacon is what goes trackside to transmit a signal as the kart passes in order to track lap time. It is generally mounted on a tripod, providing the necessary height adjustment. The beacon can have different settings so it can function for different karts on the track.

Installation of a data acquisition system

In this section we will run through the installation of a complete data acquisition system. For this example, we are using the MyChron Gold from Aim Sports. Most units are very similar in design and installation. This procedure can be used as a guideline for any type or model of system that you may be using. Always consult your owner's manual for exact installation instructions and set-up.

Main Logging Unit

First, we need to mount the main unit in order to establish a point of reference for all the sensors we will be installing. In most applications the best place to mount the logging unit is under the front fairing. It has a large flat surface, provides protection against debris and is rubber mounted to help minimize vibration.

Your unit will have four points of contact that need to be marked and drilled for the mounting hardware. The hardware is small and will require some patience to work with. Try to use rubber washers to help further isolate vibration to the main unit.

The bolts should be snug. Be careful not to over tighten, as you could crack the plastic outer casing of the main unit. Make sure you have the unit pointed in the proper direction as indicated by the manufacturer. This is important with a unit that has an accelerometer to ensure accurate readings.

Dash Display

This will be the easiest part of your installation, as the display is designed to mount directly onto the steering wheel. Some data acquisition manufacturers have special steering wheels that mount the dash display right inside the steering wheel. Most displays have a mounting bolt built into the back. Place the bolt through the top hole on the steering wheel spoke.

Make sure your steering wheel is installed properly, with one spoke pointing upward. If your steering wheel does not have any holes in the spokes you will need to mark and drill a hole. You want the dash to sit high on the wheel but not in the way of your hands or your vision.

Rear wheel speed sensor.

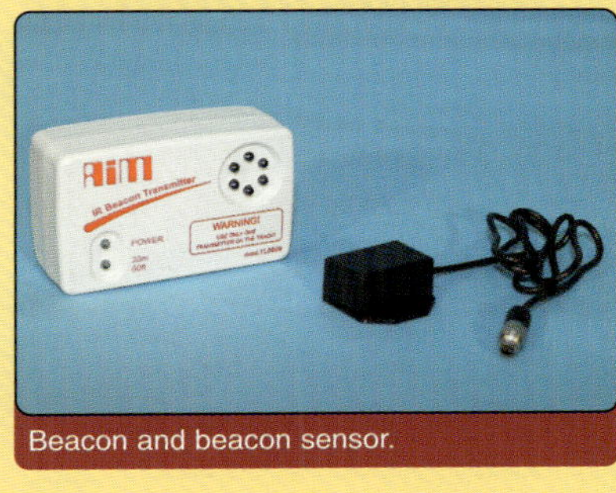

Beacon and beacon sensor.

cool trick

Mark the holes and drill for the unit from the top of the faring. This makes it easy to center the unit and can be done with the fairing left in place.

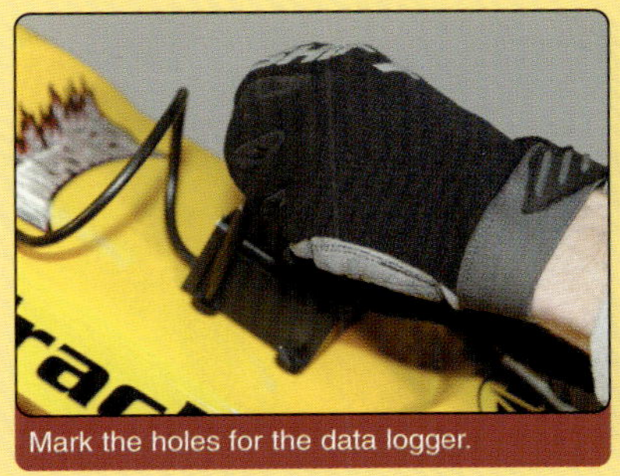

Mark the holes for the data logger.

Mount logger unit under fairing.

Make sure dash display is visible.

cool trick

When the beacon sensor is mounted on top of the front faring, drill two holes so you can switch from side to side depending on where the beacon is placed.

Ensure beacon sensor is secure.

Group extra wire together with a wrap.

Clip RPM sensor to plug wire.

Make sure you use all the proper hardware supplied, including the rubber or plastic washer. Snug the Nylock nut in place. You do not want your dash flopping around, but be careful not to over tighten. Keep the wire lead clear of the shift lever and the clutch lever. Use the front fairing mounting bracket as your pathway for the connecting wire.

Beacon Sensor

The important consideration when mounting the beacon sensor is keeping it clear of any obstructions, such as the driver's knees, which can get in the way. Many times the beacon can be placed on either side of the track so you need to spin your beacon sensor around to point at the beacon. A great way to mount your beacon sensor is with Velcro.

In the right situation, the sensor can be mounted right on the main unit, pointing over the driver's legs. Make sure you are not interfering with the flow of the steering wheel and not chaffing the sensor lead wire.

Engine Speed

The RPM, or engine speed, is the next sensor to mount. This lead will need to flow from the main unit, down the right side to the spark plug lead wire. Take a few minutes to plan out the route carefully. From the main unit, head down the right side of the steering column support post, to the frame rail. Loop the lead up to the spark plug wire and clip the sensor in place. Keep clear of the exhaust pipe and the magneto. Use small tye wraps to hold it in place.

Wheel Speed

The next sensor to install will be MPH or wheel speed. For this example we are mounting to the rear of a kart with a 50mm axle. From the main unit, head down the left side of the steering column support post, to the frame rail. Keep clear of the radiator hoses and watch for sharp edges.

Mount the sensor "L" bracket to the left side bearing cassette. Remove the hub and axle keys and then slide on the collar. Line up the collar with the sensor. Adjust the sensor pick-up to have about 1/16" or 2mm of clearance and use the lock nuts to hold the sensor in place. Do not tye wrap the wheel speed lead in place yet. We will run the temperature lead in the same direction and can combine the two, making for a nice neat installation.

Water Temperature

For this example we will be installing the inline sensor. From the main unit follow the same path as the speed sensor lead. Run the lead to the water hose that runs across the back of the seat. Cut the hose and mount the inline sensor coupling. Use hose clamps to secure the coupling in place. The sensor can then be screwed into the coupling and tightened using the jam nut. You will want to use Teflon tape or fitting sealer on the threads of the sensor to ensure you do not leak any water.

Go back and tye wrap the wheel speed lead and the water temperature lead in place. Use fuel line or automotive style wiring cover to protect the leads from chaffing.

Software

The final step is to install the software in your laptop and calibrate the system in order to establish a baseline. Some calibration can be done through the onboard dash display. You will need to input things like engine temperature range, wheel size and RPM range in order to calculate the proper outputs. With the data acquisition unit now installed, we need to understand some basic parameters in order to establish our baseline for reading.

First we need to set up the temperature range, that is the minimum and maximum temperatures we want the engine to operate at while we are racing. The water temperature should be 100° F to 135° F or 38° C to 57° C. The engine or head temperature should be 120° F to 155° F or 49° C to 68° C. The minimum and maximum ranges will set off the warning lights and show up on the analysis software. Remember to consult your engine builder regarding the temperature settings for your engine. If the temperature is too low, add tape to the radiator. If the temperature is too high, remove any tape or get a bigger radiator.

The engine speed or RPM needs to be set at this time. Most dash units use warning lights in 500 RPM increments. For most moto engines use a min of 9,000 and a max of 14,000 RPM. For ICC engines use a min of 9,000 and a max of 15,000 RPM.

It is important to understand where you hit the max RPM to understand if you could use a different gear. If you hit max RPM too early, you may want a taller gear ratio. If you hit max RPM too late, you may want to put in a shorter gear ratio. We will talk about gear ratios in more detail in chapter nine.

Now the wheel speed needs to be set up. With this we need to set the tire size, by measuring the circumference of the rear wheel. Make sure the tire is at the HOT tire pressure to ensure that the circumference is accurate. With these two values entered into the system, the data acquisition system will be able to calibrate the overall kart speed.

Split Times

If you have a number of beacons set out, breaking the track into different sections, you can evaluate split times. This will give you an indication of your performance under different conditions on the track. Multiple beacons are used by data acquisition systems that do not have track mapping capabilities. These systems rely on the beacon sensor marking the time as you pass each beacon.

Some systems use metal strips imbedded in the track. The beacon sensor uses a magnet installed in the floor pan of the kart. It will trip each time you cross the metal strip. If your system has track mapping built into the main unit, you can use the analysis software to do the same thing.

Baseline – Where do you start!

Start by looking at RPM and MPH to determine if a gear change or a jetting adjustment should be made. If, for instance, you know that your engine makes peak power at 13,000 RPM and you are showing only 12,500 RPM at the end of the straightaway, a change needs to be made. After making the appropriate gearing change, you can compare the RPM and MPH, then use your computer to determine if the now higher RPM is giving you a faster top speed.

hot tip

Wiring needs to be snug with a little room to move so you do not stress the connectors.

Align axle collar with speed sensor.

Mount inline sensor with proper clamps.

cool trick

Place the ends of those hard to stretch rubber lines into a cup of very hot water to make them easier to work with and stretch over fittings. When the rubber cools it makes a great seal.

Download cable for laptop.

Input base line system settings.

hot tip

Keep an eye on where the fuel tank overflow hose is pointing. Many times it will point in the direction of the main unit. If the fuel tank should overflow it would pour fuel onto the main unit and cause extensive corrosion of the plastic case and wire leads.

Again, I will stress the fact that consistency is key to reading data. You need to read through the data to make sure that other things like wind or a better cornering speed were not giving you a false reading. It is difficult to use the information provided by a data acquisition system to make chassis changes. That said, we could look at section times to understand if a chassis change needs to be made.

After a day on the track you will have a ton of new data to evaluate and digest. Using track-mapping information, you can analyze your performance over several laps and compare that to qualifying or practice sessions.

Reading data and actually being able to analyze it takes a lot of practice. When using your system, I would recommend just trying to analyze the basics at first. When you feel comfortable with the basics you can slowly begin to use other areas of the data software. Never spend so much time analyzing data that you don't have time to maintain or prepare your kart for the next session.

Keep an eye on all the setting changes to the baseline set up. This means as you change tires, axles and engine parts, make the proper notes on your system. This will allow you to better compare the data.

Keeping it clean

Your system has been designed to deal with elements like dirt, dust and rain. You need to keep it clean to ensure it operates consistently all the time. Try to avoid grease and grime stains on your display unit. Try to use care in keeping the dash buttons free from build up. Grease and fuel will penetrate the buttons and can lead to problems over time.

Use mild cleaners to wipe the dash, leads and sensors clean of all grime and dirt. Consult your owner's manual for all cleaning tips. Use the cleaning process to look over the nuts and bolts, checking tightness. Look at all the leads for any chaffing or cracking.

TIRE SET-UP

Bridgestone Racing go kart tires.

Rear, rain and front rims.

Rim for front spindle hub.

Rim with front bearing built in.

It is all about tires

If you have ever watched any racing on TV, you know how important tires are to the handling of a racecar. It seems you always hear comments like, “He used up his tires,” in relation to how poorly a driver is doing. It’s no different in shifter kart racing. Tires have the biggest impact on handling and lap times. Keeping this in mind, it is important to make sure that you learn to use tires to their fullest potential. By taking care of your tires, you can have an advantage over other competitors.

Like a racecar, the tires on a shifter kart are tube-less, that is, the air is held inside the tire with a tight seal between the tire bead and the wheel rim. Shifter karts use slicks for dry weather and grooved tires for wet weather. When you look at the size of a kart tire in relation to the overall weight of the kart, you get a good understanding of why shifter karts perform so well. The combination of being lightweight and having a lot of rubber makes for high levels of grip.

Rims are also a key component of the entire wheel assembly. They can be made from stamped aluminum, machined from billet stock or cast from magnesium. The high amount of grip generated by shifter karts puts a tremendous strain on the rims. Balancing weight and strength is a big factor, as rim failure will put you out of the race.

Racing kart tires are low and wide, compared to other racing tires. The aspect ratio, or relationship of height to tread width, is between 36% and 37%. Formula 1 tires are 45%. This allows a kart to have a short side wall, which creates a tire that reacts quickly to driver input.

The tread is the section that contacts the road. It is made up of a thin layer of rubber, which is bonded to the carcass. It is the compound or formulation of this rubber that determines the grip and wear characteristics.

The carcass is the main part of the tire. It is made up of a bias or diagonal overlap of nylon cord layers. The angle of the layers, cord size and sidewall stiffness determine the tire’s response and ride nature.

The bead area is a bundle of steel wires that strengthen the carcass where it meets the rim. This forms the air seal and, because of its stiffness, makes mounting and removing the tires difficult.

In this chapter we will look at how to mount and dismount tires, break in new tires and set tire pressures for racing. A durometer gauge, pyrometer, air pressure gauge and a tape measure are the tools you need to make the proper tire pressure decisions.

How a kart tire works

Basically, a kart tire relies on the relationship between heat and air pressure to perform at its optimum level. The heat is generated by the sidewall flexing and by the contact patch scrubbing on the track surface. As the temperature builds inside the tire, the air temperature goes up and the tire pressure increases. The tire pressure itself can also be a factor in heat build-up in a race tire. Tire temperature determines the grip and rolling resistance of the tire.

The numbers that describe the tire are stamped into the sidewall. For example an 11 x 6.00-5 tire is the dimensional size of the tire in inches. The first number, 11, indicates the height of the tire, in this case, 11 inches tall, which is also 11 inches in diameter. The next number, 7.10, indicates the tread width or contact area which in our example is 7.1 inches wide. The last number, 5, designates a rim size of 5 inches.

Each tire will have a directional arrow indicator. It is important to understand that this is the direction of the tire for acceleration. For rear tires this should be pointing forward or the normal direction of forward movement. However, for front tires on a 125 cc shifter kart, this should be pointing backwards because braking forces are opposite to acceleration forces.

Tire compounds vary and are usually determined in the class rules. If choosing a tire compound, soft compounds are best suited to racing on tracks where the surface is very cold or slippery. Harder compounds work better in warm, summer weather. Often clubs will designate harder compounds which are designed to last a long time and help keep costs down.

Durometer is the measure of the rubber compound. Too hard a compound means that the racer is sacrificing grip. Grip controls both forward traction as well as sideslip of the kart. Tires are all rated with a compound designation. Tire manufacturers tell us how the compound code relates to a numeric value that ranges from 1 to 100. You can test a tire's durometer using an analog gauge with a test probe. Try to be very consistent in your test process so that the readings can be compared to other readings that you have taken or will take in the future.

Before you check the durometer, the first step is to determine the temperature of the tires that you will be testing. A tire that has been exposed to the sun, or a tire that has just come off a racetrack will likely have a lower durometer reading than the same tire when it is allowed to cool down.

Be sure to evaluate the available tread depth when you are using your durometer gauge to evaluate tires. A tire with very little tread will have a higher durometer reading. Apply a firm but even pressure as you put the durometer gauge to the tire. If the tire is used, it is a good idea to be sure that you have used a scraper to remove any dirt or stones, which may have adhered to the tire as the driver drove into the pits.

Record the reading, including the temperature, into your logbook or laptop computer. Remember, soft tires have low numbers on the durometer gauge. That indicates that these tires are likely to have a great deal of grip but they are also likely to have very poor durability. Tires with low numbers will wear rapidly.

Once you have your readings then you are ready to match up sets of tires. You should have a tape measure to check the circumference of the tire. The circumference is only valid if the tire is mounted on the wheel and the tire is inflated to the HOT pressure that would be used for racing.

If you have purchased tires from your local kart shop and the wrap is discolored from exposure to the sun, it is possible that you will find a tire, which is quite inconsistent from a hardness perspective. If one side has been repeatedly exposed to the sun while the other side of the tire has always remained shielded from the sun, the exposed portion is likely to be harder than the portion which remained in the shade.

Mounting Shifter Kart Tires

Anyone who has ever tried to mount a tire on a one-piece wheel rim will be able to confirm that this can be a daunting task. Getting the

Rear and front tire height.

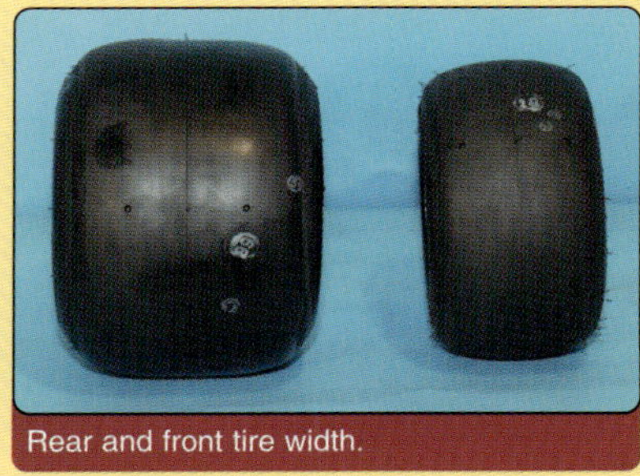
Rear and front tire width.

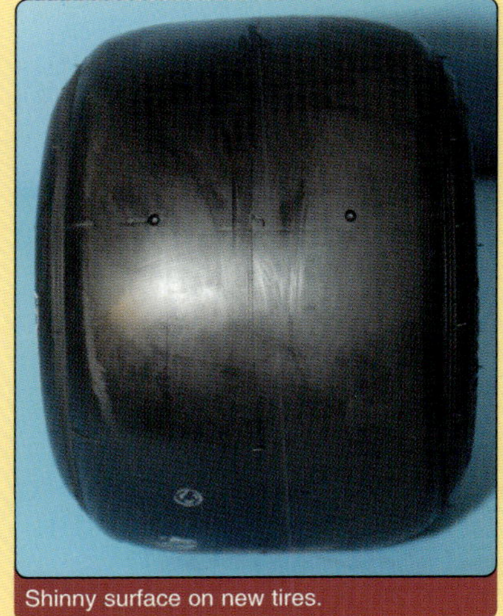
Shinny surface on new tires.

Measuring the tire run-out.

cool trick

To mount your tires with the wrappers left on, you need to cut back some of the wrapper. Very carefully, using a sharp knife, cut back 1" all the way around.

Cutting the wrapper with a razor.

Removing wrapper edge before mounting.

stiff rubber of the tire bead over the edges of the wheel rim is often exceedingly difficult. With proper technique and a lot of practice you can mount tires quickly and painlessly. With practice, how fast should you expect it to take? Without rushing, it usually takes me no more than five minutes to dismount an old set and mount up a new set of tires.

Following the steps outlined below will make mounting the tires somewhat easier. Don't try to do the tire mounting on a hard surface, like concrete or asphalt, since you might damage the tire or rim. Having a piece of carpet is good, because it is soft enough that neither tire nor rim will be scratched or damaged and it will allow the tire-rim combination to get some grip during the mounting process. For our example we are mounting a set of Bridgestone tires on a set of Douglas rims.

First, identify the smaller edge of the wheel rim. Most often it's the inside of the wheel rim, or the side that does not contain the valve. Some types of rims like Douglas Wheels seem to have equally sized lips on both sides. However, when you look closely at the edge of the inside lip, you can probably see that the lip is somewhat thinner, and that its edge is more rounded. So, even in the case of equally sized lips, the inside lip is still a little easier to slip the tire over.

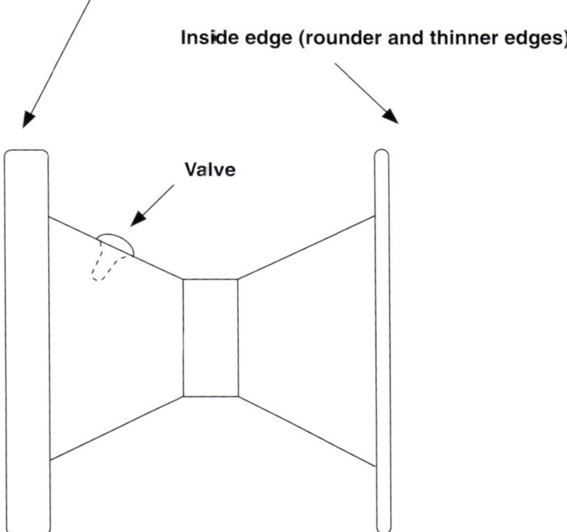

Now place the tire on the ground and lube the outer edge of the tire and the bottom edge of the rim. Be sure the lube will not damage the rubber of the tire. Mild cleaner like Simple Green is best for this. Dish washing liquid is quite popular along with other products like WD40. Whatever you do, choose something slippery that can be washed off and does not damage the rubber of the tire. Be sure to apply plenty of lube all around, but make sure you do not splash it into the inside of the tire. Excess fluid in the tire will have a negative affect on the amount of tire pressure variance. Keep the lube close by, since you might need it again later.

Now kneel down, with the tire flat on the ground. Press the rim down onto the tire on an angle, so that the rim makes contact with the tire bead on two points. Now twist the rim while you apply pressure, trying to get the rim to slip into that part of the tire.

During this process, you might find that the tire collapses, turning inside out. Putting pressure on the tire in between your knees while pushing the tire in will help to keep this from happening. With your hands you will find you can roll or twist the rim into the tire.

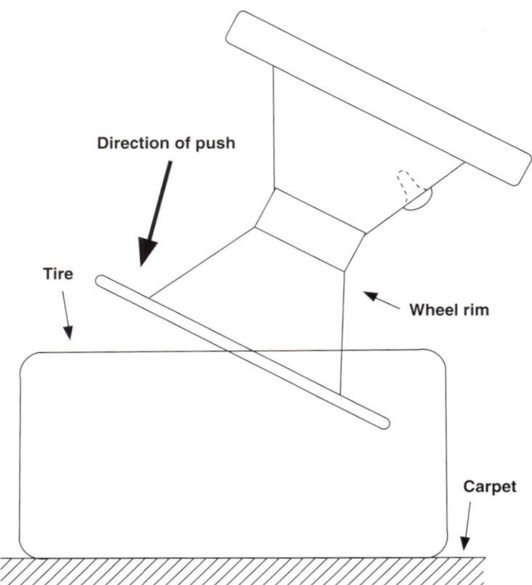

Now for the other side of the tire. Flip the wheel over so the rim is now on the floor. Apply some more lube of your choice to the edge of the rim. Now grip the tire very firmly, putting your whole weight behind it. Eventually it should slip on, just the same as the first bead. You may find that you need to grab each side and roll the bead onto the rim.

If your rims have bead locks, now is the time to install them. Make sure they are clean and have a rubber O-ring in good condition. Put them in until they are just past flush. You should be able to pass your finger over the hole and just feel the tip of the bead lock. If you put them in too far the tire will have difficulty seating. If you do not put them in far enough the hole can fill with the rubber from the bead itself. Taking extreme care with bead locks is important. Bead locks generally do not have much thread to start with and are prone to leaking and stripping.

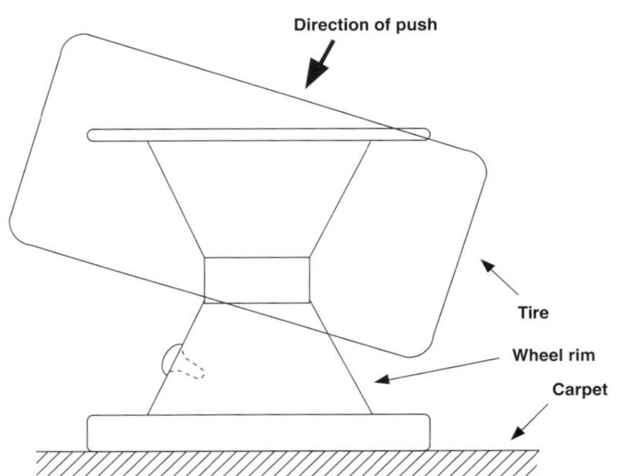

warning

In general, during all of these procedures, keep your face, hands, etc. as far away as possible from the tire. Always wear safety glasses.

Lube tire and rim to make it easier.

Roll the rim into the tire.

Roll the bead onto the rim.

hot tip

If the tire bead will not seat, you can help it by tying a broad belt very, very tightly around the circumference of the tire. This will squeeze the outside surface of the tire together, which will squeeze the bead tighter around the rim and make for easier sealing.

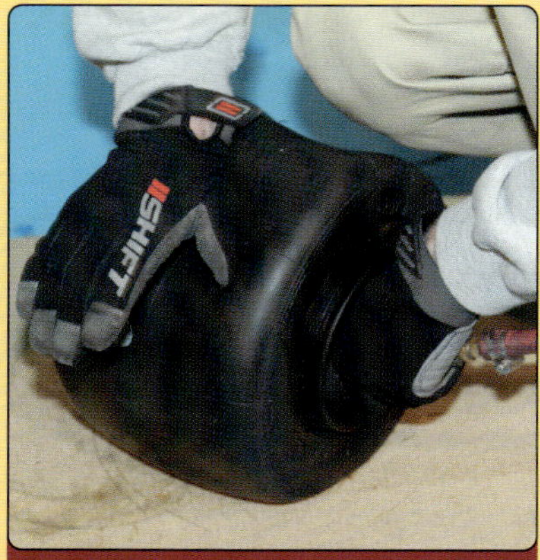

Use air to close the gap.

warning

Inflating tires bears the risk of serious property damage and/or injury. Always wear safety glasses.

warning

Be careful when using high-pressure compressed air. Faulty tires may explode if the pressure gets too high. Use a safety cage when ever inflating tires past the recommended tire pressures.

When you have just mounted a tire on a rim, you might notice that there is actually a gap between the tire bead and the wheel rim. When inflating the tires, it is important to get the seal as tight as possible or you will have a difficult time getting the bead to seat. Using a compressor, force air in at such a high rate, that it cannot escape from the gap fast enough. The tire will rapidly expand until it reaches the rim providing the desired seal. The valve core can resist the fast inflation, so it may be necessary to remove the valve core.

As you inflate the tire, the pressure will grow, and the tire's bead will start to slide up the rim. Applying plenty of lube can help reduce the friction between the rubber and rim material. When you apply high pressures (40 or 50 psi), you may exceed the recommendations of the manufacturer.

Take all safety precautions. Use a long air chuck to give you some safety distance. It is recommended that you put your tires into a safety cage to seat the beads. If you are unsure about seating your tires see your local dealer.

When a bead seats under high pressure, it can produce a loud metallic sounding POP. Don't be alarmed, that's normal. One bead often seats much earlier than the second bead, so keep increasing the pressure. Eventually, the second bead will seat, again with a loud POP. Be careful not to get your fingers between the wheel lip and the tire bead when the bead seats. The pressure is capable of seriously squishing your fingers. Make sure your fingers are nowhere near the tire and rim when you are trying to seat the bead.

Once both beads are seated, check that they have even contact with the lip of the wheel rim. To keep from over stretching the tire, reduce the air pressure back to the HOT pressure. To complete the installation process, tighten the bead locks. Make sure you check the bead locks for air leaks by spraying them with soapy water and looking for bubbles.

Choosing the Right Pressure

New tires all need a little break in time before they are able to reach optimum grip levels. Tires have a slick surface on them when they are new. This surface coating is a seal to keep the rubber fresh and protect the tire from contaminates. A coating of mold release is also on the outer surface of the tire and is very slippery. This will make the first few turns on your new tires very slick. Try not to excessively slide the kart or spin the wheels until the grip level comes up. Every heat cycle on tires makes them harder, so you want to bring the temperature up slowly to ensure proper break in. Too much heat too fast can shorten the life of the tires.

Once you have scrubbed your tires and brought them up to temperature, pull into the pits and check your tire pressures HOT. We want to set the tire pressures HOT because this is where the tires operate on the track. It is also important to note the differences between your starting COLD and your actual HOT tire pressures.

Proper pressure is difficult to generalize because it can vary with driver, chassis, track layout, road surface, weather and temperature. A good starting point for your tire pressures are 10 psi at the front and 13 psi at the rear for a soft compound tire. Remember, you generally want to have 2 to 3 lbs more air in the rear than in the front because the volume of air in the tire is so much less in the smaller front tire. Most manufacturers have an approved range of 10 psi to 25 psi.

For medium compound tires use a front/rear COLD pressure of 12/15 psi and 18/23 psi for hard compound tires as a baseline from which to adjust. Remember these are COLD tire pressures. The HOT pressures should be 2 to 3 psi higher. Make adjustments to your COLD pressure to ensure you hit the optimum HOT pressure. Because the tire pressure is important to performance, an accurate gauge is essential.

Outside temperature change has a big impact on tire pressure. The general rule is to raise pressure during the cool part of the day. This will decrease the contact patch and generate more heat sooner. As the day warms up (noon), you can decrease the pressure by 1 to 3 psi. The lower pressure will decrease heat build-up.

You should be aware of your race pressure from practice. Race pressure lets you run at your optimum lap time for enough laps to last the race. Too high a tire pressure and you build up too much heat too quickly causing the tires to lose grip. Too low a starting pressure and the tires will lack grip at the beginning of the race. You can run mock races in practice to find the right starting pressure, making sure you always check the pressure hot. Check the pressures when the tires have cooled down and make a note of both the HOT and COLD pressures in your logbook.

It is possible to adjust tire pressures to help fix a handling problem. For one, air pressure has a big effect on the stability of your kart. If you have excessive hopping, you can try adding slightly more tire pressure to settle the kart down. Adding a substantial amount of tire pressure will take away grip from that tire. So, if you have a push, adding more pressure in the rear will take away grip and give the kart a better balance. Again, I would never recommend this as a long-term fix to a problem. Your goal is to get the tires to work at their maximum grip level and then to get your kart handling tuned to be able to use that grip. You should only use tire pressures to help handling when tiny changes need to be made.

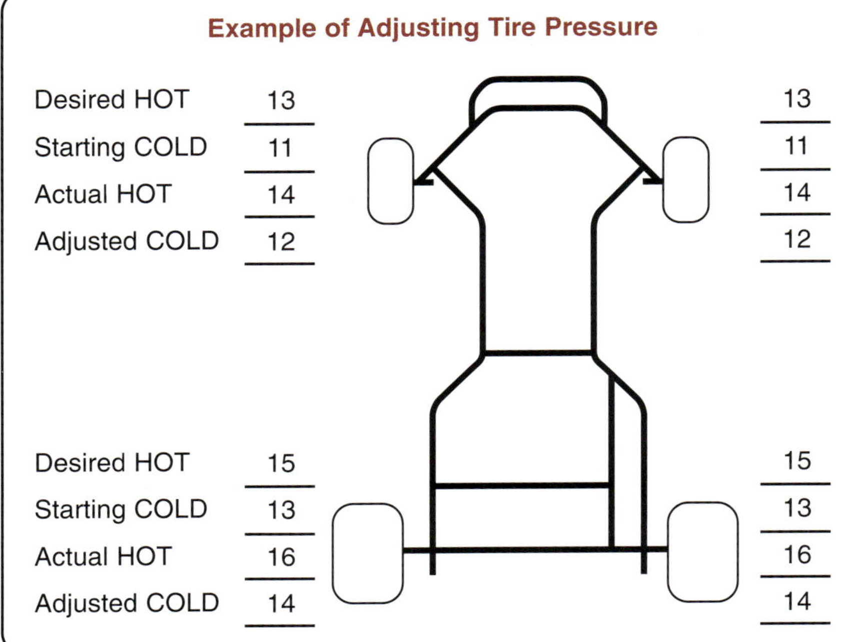

Set your tire pressures immediately.

New tire and scuffed tire surfaces.

hot tip

In single lap qualifying, put a little extra pressure in your tires. This will build up the heat faster, creating more grip for the short qualifying session.

Removing the air form the wheel.

Breaking the tire bead.

Using irons to remove the tire.

Lifting the rim out with irons.

Watch for the tire to shred or get tiny little cuts or splits in the surface. This may be a sign that the tire is overheated. The tire should have a pebbled look to it. If the tire overheats even once, it will suffer a significant amount of deterioration in grip next time you run.

Removal and Storage

Dismounting old tires can be as much of a chore as mounting new tires. We will talk about removing the old tires with and without tire irons. Although it is much more difficult to remove a tire without tire irons, it is always preferred. Even being very careful, using tire irons will mark the rim, which can damage new tires and make mounting more difficult.

First, to remove tires with tire irons, remove the air using a Philips screwdriver by pressing in the valve core. For best results, choose a screwdriver size that fits the valve stem perfectly. If you have bead locks on your rims remove them.

Next, break the bead using a bead breaker. There are a number of manual units on the market. In our example we are using a unit from RLV. Break the bead on the inside first, then the outside or valve stem side. With both beads now off the lip of the rim place the rim, valve stem side down on a piece of old carpet.

Now, push one edge of the tire to the narrow middle of the rim. Take the tire iron and place it on the other side and pull down. Take the other iron and do the same. Be careful as the tire iron can stretch or mark the bead area. Remember the bead is made up of steel strands and if it gets bent or stretched it can be hard to set the bead. When removing the old tires to be discarded we do not care about the bead area but we do want to be careful with the rim.

With the tire irons in place, try to pull the tire over the rim to about half way. The rest of the tire should pop off. Now flip the tire over. The other edge of the rim can be pulled off by hand.

Now, let's look at how to remove a tire without using tire irons. The first step is to break the bead as outlined above. Then, with the inside of the tire, roll the top of the tire inwards. This will make the bottom tire bead extend itself over the rim. Now, grab the extended bead and slowly work the tire off the rim until the entire bead has been removed over the rim.

Now, flip over the tire and rim and angle the rim into the carpet while putting pressure on the top of the rim with your left hand. Take your right hand and use your palm to slowly work the outside bead over the inside surface of the rim. Although this technique takes a little practice, it will keep your rims free of marks from using tire irons.

Before using the rim again, check for dents, cracks and bends. File off any burrs or marks, especially on the lip where the bead makes contact. With magnesium rims check for cracks. Throw out damaged rims as they can ruin a good set of tires or fail under pressure. Clean the rim with contact or brake cleaner. Make sure you remove any rubber that is stuck to the bead seating area. Rims should be stored in a safe place to avoid being banged around. Small nicks and marks on the lip can make sealing difficult.

Taking care of your tires off the track is very often overlooked. Once you have run your tires you have broken the outer seal. This seal keeps the rubber fresh and protects the surface against contaminates like gas, oil and cleaners. You need to wrap your tires in plastic wrap and put them in a dark bag or a rack in your trailer. This will keep the environment and sunlight from drying out and hardening the rubber. This is especially important for club racers who use a hard compound tire that is raced on more than once. Also, this is good for race tires that can be used for practice.

With practice and patience tires become less of a mystery. Do not be afraid to work with your tires and keep good notes on pressures and changes.

Warning

Screwdrivers are not tire irons. They can mark the rim. Also they can break and cause serious damage. Use only recommended tire irons.

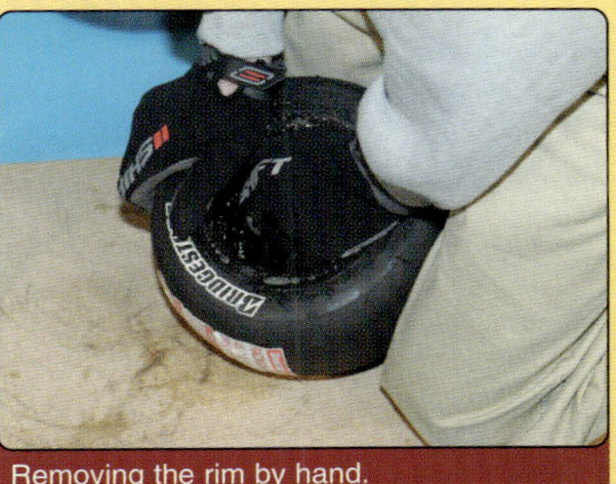

Removing the rim by hand.

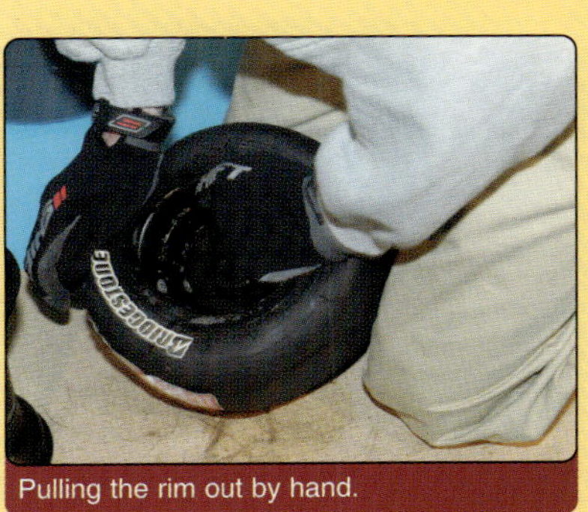

Pulling the rim out by hand.

BALANCE SET-UP

Prepping your kart for balancing.

Finding the Right Balance

Putting your kart on scales is perhaps the most important thing you can do to ensure the proper handling of your shifter kart. It is really the final touch after you have set up the chassis, mounted the seat and installed the engine. When the kart is put on the scales and balanced, you are ensuring that the proper overall weight and ideal weight distribution is achieved. As a result, the kart will have the potential to perform to its optimum level.

Before you begin to race, you need to make sure that the weight is properly distributed to the four corners of the kart. The balancing process is actually measuring the amount of weight that each tire is bearing. Scaling will also provide some tell-tale signs that your set-up is not accurate or your chassis is bent. The scaling process is a great baseline check of the entire kart and can often uncover problems before they become serious.

Far too often a driver will spend a lot of time and money building a faster engine, buying a new chassis or mounting new tires, when more time could be gained by balancing the kart correctly. Your chassis manufacturer or local dealer should have the specifications and guidelines for correct weight distribution for your kart.

Removing the front brake calipers.

Why is kart balancing so important to the overall performance of a kart? In chapter three we learned that a kart must lack weight from the inside rear tire to the outside rear tire in order to efficiently turn through a corner. This weight transfer is helped by the geometry of the front of the kart and the flex of the chassis. In order to accomplish this weight transfer evenly and effectively, we need to begin with a kart that is properly balanced. That is, a kart that has the overall weight distributed evenly.

As we learned in chapter four on seat set-up, the overall design of a chassis is meant to help compensate for the weight of the engine by placing the seat to the left of centre. The proper seat installation may result in almost perfect weight distribution before any extra weight is added to the kart. The other benefit of scaling your kart is that you can get a clearer understanding of exactly how much the kart weighs with the driver. You can then determine how much weight needs to be added to meet class weight minimums.

Kart Preparation

A number of clear steps need be taken in order to properly balance your kart. These include doing a front-end alignment, looking at the tire run-out, checking ride height and setting the fluid levels. It is vital that the kart be square, that is the same chassis settings on both sides. If it is not, then it will not matter how much time you spend setting the front-end alignment, the kart will always want to steer better in one direction.

Pulling off the front spindles.

Front-End Alignment

Begin by putting the kart up on a stand and removing the front wheels, hubs and in the case of 80cc karts, the wheel spacers. For 125cc karts, you will need to remove the outer hub, which means pulling off the front brake calipers.

The first thing you need to do is to check the front spindles. Start by making sure that the spindles are tight but not rigid. They must turn easily from side to side. Excessive sloppiness in the spindles is a sign that the bearings are worn out. Replace the bearings before moving to the next step.

Next, we will check that the spindle height is set equally on both sides. The number of spacers above and below the spindle should be the same because the height will affect the actual corner weights. Also, we need to check the caster and camber. Look to see that the caster and camber is set equal on both sides. If you have a standard pill with no adjustment you should be ok. If you have an adjustable pill, set them to the same position.

Setting the front-end alignment and then locking the steering in place is a critical part of scaling your kart. After making sure all your geometry settings are symmetrical, you need to check for toe alignment. A misaligned front-end will give you false corner weight readings.

Start by centering the steering shaft straight ahead. Remember, the steering shaft is offset to the left or brake side. This offset will make visually aligning the steering shaft a more difficult task than it sounds. Special care should be taken to make sure that it is done correctly.

With the steering shaft pointed straight ahead, the next step is to lock the steering shaft in place. I've found that the best place to do this is at the base of the shaft using a pair of locking pliers so that the handles are positioned in a way that they won't move. Make sure you mark this position with a marker or a scribe so you can see if the steering moves during the set-up process.

To properly set your front toe it is best to use an alignment tool kit such as the Exact-Toe from RLV. An alignment tool is critical. You cannot eyeball the alignment because a chassis is not symmetrical. If one wheel is slightly angled it will provide a different weight reading. Being precise and accurate is critical at this stage.

Now place the alignment end plates on the stub axles, check for level and tighten the end plate bolts. Put the Exact-Toe bar in place and take a reading. Loosen the jam nuts on the tie rods and make sure the tie rods turn easily. Remember that the threads on the tie rods and hemispherical joints are right and left threaded. Make sure you are careful not to strip a nut going in the wrong direction. Double check to make sure your steering wheel is centered and pointed straight ahead as marked earlier. Turn the tie rods forward or backward to move the spindles to identical settings on the Exact Toe end plates. As a baseline, set the toe at 1/16" to 1/8" toe out. Keep in mind, when the kart is set on the ground and the driver gets in, the extra weight will move the tires in.

Now we need to look at the camber settings. Equal camber settings are very important because camber directly affects the height of each corner. Camber can be checked with the Exact Toe alignment tool. Loosen the end plate bolts, drop the end plates down vertically, check for level and tighten the bolts. Then slip the Exact Toe bar in and check the camber. It should be set equally.

If either the caster or camber do not measure equally with the same setting on the frame, it may be a sign that either your spindle or frame are bent. For slight variances, it is ok to have different adjustments side to side in order to arrive at the same caster or camber reading. For major differences, consult your chassis maufacturer or dealer.

Lining up the steering column.

Locking the steering shaft in place.

hot tip

Make sure your tie rods move in the same direction. That is if you turn the left one forward and the spindle moves out, the right tie rod will do the same. This makes it less confusing when adjusting.

Check the exact size of each tire.

Level the alignment plate.

Insert the alignment bar.

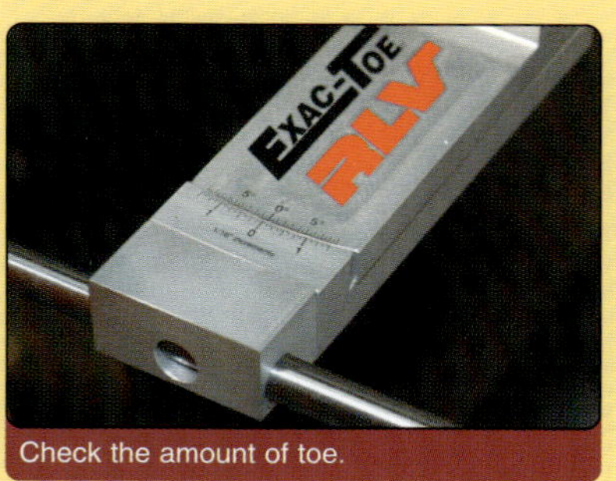

Check the amount of toe.

Tire Run out

Put your tires back on and inflate them to the proper HOT pressures. Measure the circumference or run-out of each tire to make sure, you do not have an overly large tire, which will have an impact on the weight distribution. Take a thin, flexible 1/4" tape measure, wrap it around the middle of the tire and read the measurement.

Make sure the tires are free of any debris such as stones or hay that may affect the measurement. If one tire is considerably bigger than the other adjust the air pressure to close the difference. This may mean a little less pressure in one tire and a little extra pressure in the other tire. The scale doesn't care about tire pressure, only circumference. If equal circumference with your tires cannot be achieved by adjusting pressure, you may have to mount another tire.

Fluid Levels

When scaling your kart leave the fuel tank empty. This will ensure a consistent scaling process. When it's time to scale your kart again, you won't have to remember what level your fuel was at in your previous scaling. Another benefit of scaling with an empty tank is that if you happen to burn most of your fuel, you have the peace of mind knowing that you will not be under weight. As far as the rest of the fluids, it is important that the radiator water and the transmission oil be filled to normal operating levels.

Driver Equipment

In order to get proper weight readings, make sure you have all your driving gear on. This includes your helmet, gloves, suit, rib protector, neck collar and shoes. You want to be as close to actual race conditions as possible.

Setting the plate for checking camber.

Checking the camber angle.

Baseline Balancing

Start by placing your scales on a level floor. Measure the width and length of the kart to get a sense of how far apart the scales need to be. You need to make sure the scales are exactly level. This can be done by using a long level and checking the floor where the centerlines of the front and rear axles will rest. You will need to compensate for an uneven floor by placing shims under the appropriate corners of the scales. Make sure the display unit is charged and ready to go.

Scaling is usually a two-man job, and enlisting a friend to help is important. Make sure you have your scaling chart ready from page 118 of the Appendix. Have extra copies on hand. Also, make sure you have a copy of the rules book with your class weight in it. Test the scales by standing on each one individually and noting any difference between the scales. Ideally, the weight should be identical.

Next, place the kart carefully on the scales, making sure the wheels are centered on each scale pad. If the wheels are not centered during weighing, you may not get an accurate reading. Have your helper hold the front of the kart and pull the brake on, as you carefully get into position. When sitting in the kart, apply the brake to keep the kart from rolling off the scales. It is important to maintain a normal driving position including your arms, hands and posture.

Setting up the scaling pads.

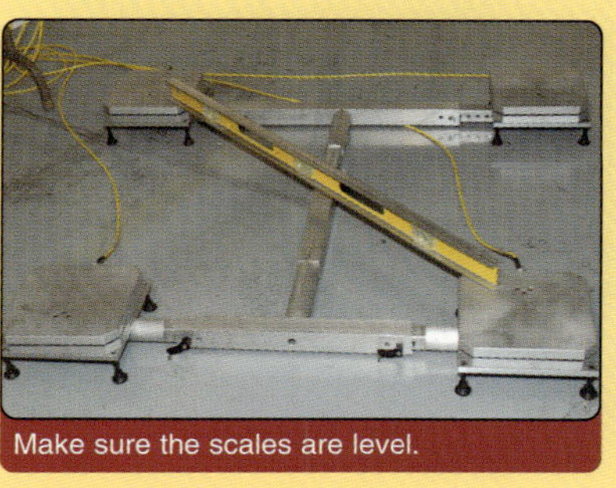
Make sure the scales are level.

Adjusting Kart Balance

Kart corner weights are usually not at the desired specifications after the first weighing. If you are under your specific class weight limit, add weight to the appropriate locations in order to get an equal side-to-side distribution.

The following weight distributions are recommended for most karts:

42%	Front Weight
58%	Rear Weight
50/50	Left/Right Weight

These are just recommended starting points. Weight can be moved around at the track to change the handling characteristics of the chassis and will be discussed in chapters 10 and 11.

Keep the side-to-side weight distribution as close to 50/50 as possible. If you are a long way off on your side-to-side weight distribution, you might have to move the seat to get the correct weight distribution.

Your front corner weights should be within 5 lbs. of each other, and the same applies to the rear wheels. If after adjusting the lead and seat position, this is not the case, re-check all of the factors affecting weight distribution and re-weigh. If the problem still exists, you may have a chassis problem.

When you add weight to a kart for balancing, it is important to understand some basic physics. Remember an object will stay in motion until acted upon. For this reason, it is recommended that the weight be placed as close to the center of the kart as possible, while still achieving the desired equal corner weights. Weight added outside this range requires more energy to change its direction.

Place the kart on the scale carefully.

Holding the brake for the driver.

BALANCE SET-UP

warning

Do not place lead shot inside the frame tubes to balance your kart. This type of weight will shift in the frame from the cornering forces and cause handling problems.

Imagine a huge lead weight bolted on the rear bumper. As you enter a turn the chunk of lead still wants to go straight. Some of the grip must now be used to change its direction. Once you get it moving in the right direction, you have to stop it from swinging and changing its direction again. This type of pendulum effect has a big impact on kart handling.

When placing lead on your kart it is best to start by bolting it on the seat. The best place to put it is on the left or back side of your seat, depending on your readings. I recommend using the rubber covered scuba diving weights. They come in nice easy increments, look good and are easy to handle. Weights can be frame mounted with the proper mounting brackets.

Once final weight placement is determined, secure all weight properly. The hardware will need to be at least 5/16" Grade 5 or better or 8.8 M8 bolts of the appropriate length. Be sure to cross drill and safety wire or safety clip each one. Most sanctioning bodies require double nutting of the ballast as well. Be sure to consult your rule book. Not securing your weight properly has the potential to cause injury and equipment damage and is the basis for disqualification after a race.

The balancing of your kart is not a one-time process, and should be done on a regular and frequent basis. This is especially true if you make a major change such as a new seat.

Writing down the scale readings.

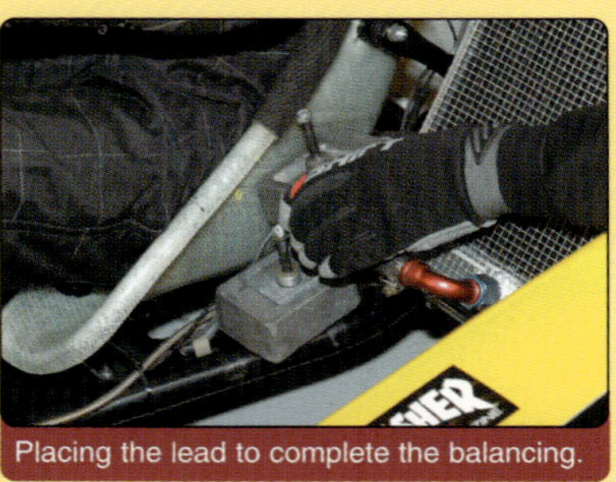
Placing the lead to complete the balancing.

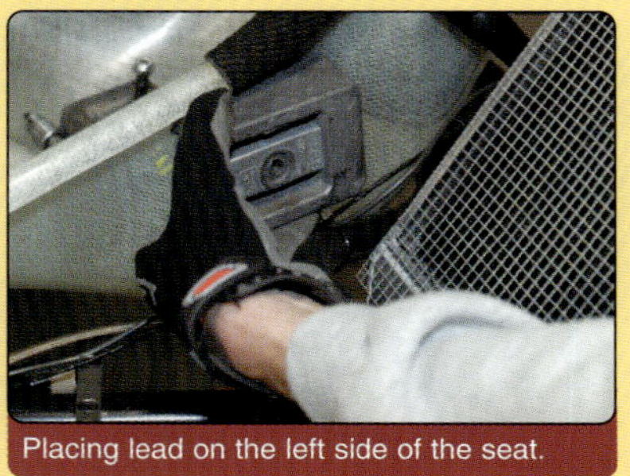
Placing lead on the left side of the seat.

Scaling Chart Sample

Scaling Chart

Date: Jan 22/03
Location: San Fran
Tire: Bridgestone YGB

Kart: Trackmagic MG
Engine: TM 125 ICC
Wheel: Douglas

Driver: Gidley
Class Weight: 385
Other: Tillett Seat

	Left	Front	Right
%	20.7	42.2	21.5
lbs/kg	80	163	83
Caster:	12		12
Toe:	0		0
Run Out:	31.0		31.0
PSI:	13		13

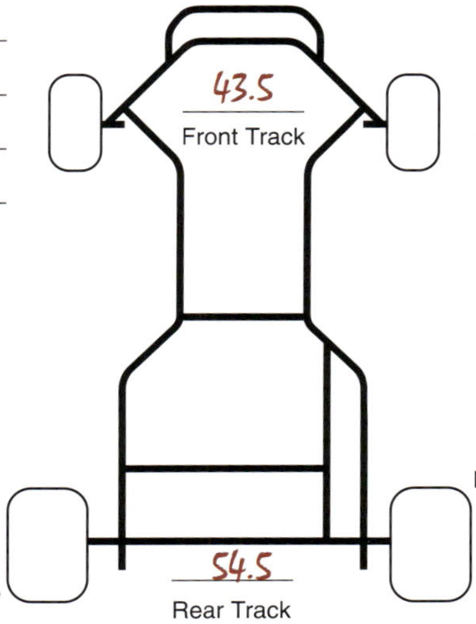

Front Track: 43.5

Draw in placement of lead.

	Left	Rear	Right
Run Out:	34.5		34.5
PSI:	15		15
%	28.7	57.8	29.1
lbs/kg	111	223	112

Rear Track: 54.5

	Left Total	Total	Right Total
%	49.5		50.5
lbs/kg	191	386	195

Notes:

Placing lead on the lower back.

Placing lead on the upper back.

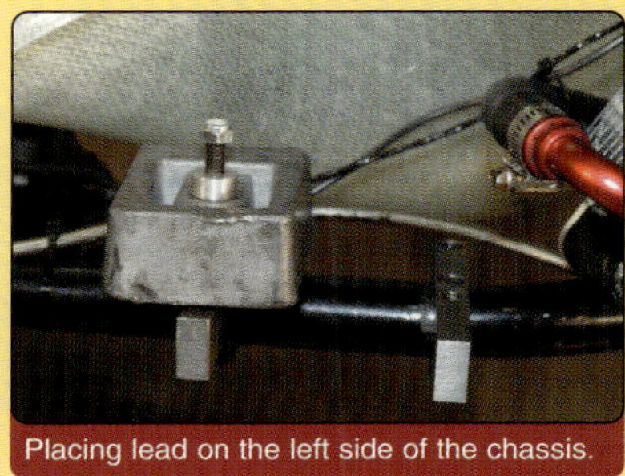
Placing lead on the left side of the chassis.

Diving weights work great.

GEARING SET-UP

Kyle Martin pulls down the straight.

Maximizing Speed

In this chapter we look at gearing your shifter kart. In all forms of kart racing gearing is important to overall lap times and to top speed. This is made even more complicated in shifter karts because the transmission introduces another dimension to the mix. No longer can we just look at the ratio between the drive sprocket and axle gear. We now need to consider the internal gear ratios in the transmission which can differ from engine manufacturer to engine manufacturer.

In all shifter kart series, changing the internal gear ratios in the transmission is not permitted. Your only means to change your gear ratios comes from the final drive sprockets. Because of this gearing limitation, you may have to give up some top speed in order to find the right gear ratio for a specific corner or series of corners. Finding the right gearing is an exercise in trial and error.

The data acquisition system we installed earlier will help us look at how our changes affect our lap times and our engine performance. Gearing is specific to each track layout and must be tuned to work with your engine set-up. As we learned in chapter five, the power band can be moved within the RPM range. Gearing affects the speed at every RPM range, so it is important to make sure these match to ensure maximum speed.

Jake Pierson powers off a corner.

Remember, you can't create horsepower by altering your gearing set-up. However, you can apply your available horsepower in the best possible way with proper testing and careful planning.

Ratios and Rotation

The basic principle of gear ratios is quite simple. The ratio is based on comparing the number of turns that the front sprocket makes versus the rear sporcket. A lower ratio, that is the front gear and the rear gear are close in size, creates high speed with low torque. With a higher ratio, the gears are much different in size, which creates more torque but will produce less top-end speed. With a shifter kart you are always looking to set the gearing for the maximum top speed, while making sure that the entire RPM range has adequate pul off the corners.

With shifter karts, what at first seems a fairly simple operation of adding or subtracting for lower or higher ratios may not be good enough. The first consideration is that we need a range of ratios not only to cover all the different racetracks, but also to allow us to fine tune throughout the day. A problem can arise because of the low numbers of teeth on shifter kart sprockets and gears. It can be difficult to make small steps in the ratios. To enable us to calculate ratio changes and a suitable range of ratios, we must look at the entire drive train, which includes the internal gears of the transmission.

Speeding through a sweeping corner.

To be accurate it is important to relate our gearing choices to MPH. We will look at a formula that will allow us to calculate miles per hour, which is better than the decimal ratio of the final drive. Different drivers may arrive at the same MPH using different gears, because of factors such as engine type and RPM.

First, we need to gather all the necessary ratios, some of which are available from your engine supplier. The required ratios include engine primary ratio, gearbox ratios and the final drive ratio. The primary drive ratio is made up of the number of teeth on the crankshaft gear divided by the number of teeth on the gearbox input or clutch drum. For a YZ 125 that number is .297 versus a CR125 which is .300. The gearbox ratio is determined by the number of teeth on the input shaft divided by the number of teeth on the output shaft. For most shifter kart engines, sixth gear is a 1:1 ratio making this value 1. The final drive ratio is the number of teeth on the engine sprocket divided by the number of teeth on the axle gear. A 15/23 gear combination would have a value of 0.652.

With all of our ratios on hand, we can now calculate the expected speed using the following formula:

MPH = (RPM x Tire Diameter x 3.1416 x Primary Ratio x Gear Ratio x Final Drive Ratio) / 1056

The RPM you should use is the peak value for the chosen powerband. If you move your powerband down with a change in pipe or ignition timing your speed calculation will change. Next, we need to get the height of the tire as indicated on the sidewall of the tire. In most cases this will be 11.0.

So, here is a quick example based on a Yamaha YZ125 motor:

(12,500 x 11.0 x 3.1416 x .297 x 1 x 0.652) / 1056 = 79.20 MPH.

With this formula in mind we can calculate the MPH over our entire set of available final drive gear ratios. As an example, we have 16 and 17 tooth engine sprockets and 19, 20 and 21 tooth axle gears. Take each engine sprocket and divide it in turn by each axle gear. This gives us six different ratios. Now you can calculate the MPH and sort them in order from lowest to highest for a quick reference.

The difference between each ratio is far from being equal, so much so that you may find some of the ratios are almost the same, while others have a difference of between four and five MPH. A four to five MPH difference is too big a gap given the very narrow power bands used on shifter karts. It is important to have a complete selection of gear ratios to choose from.

To find out which gears you may wish to purchase, determine the perfect ratio. Take each available axle gear and multiply it by the new ratio. We are looking for a whole number as this is going to be the number of teeth in our engine sprocket. Do not expect to solve the ratio exactly, the chances of that are very small.

Understanding the MPH method is especially important when you go to a new track. Try to find out from the local drivers or the track owner what speed the top runners are hitting. This will allow you to determine what range of gears you may need before you head out. This will ensure you don't get caught without enough gearing choices.

Once you have determined your optimum gearing list, keep in mind all of your available gears. Our only interest in these gears is as a back-up for our calculated list. We have already seen that some of the ratios come very close to each other, so they could be used as spares in case of a problem. In this instance it is a good idea to take note of all the ratios in addition to the calculated list.

Rear gears can vary in size a lot.

cool trick

Here's how to calculate your wheels diameter (D) from a known circumference (C):

D= [C ÷ (2 x pi)] x 2

Pi = 3.1416

Example: Assume you have a wheel circumference you've measured at 40.85".
The wheel diameter is:
[40.85 ÷ (2 x 3.1416)] x 2 = 11"

Typical 21 to 24 tooth gear set.

Front sprocket on a TM ICC engine.

Each individual driver has different requirements and may demand finer ratio changes over a narrower MPH range. Nobody is suggesting that dozens of sprockets and gears are required. The whole idea of the calculations is to eliminate much of the trial and error and expense of buying a bunch of sprockets and gears you do not really need. The formula itself is the key to many questions. With a little juggling it can be changed to provide several different answers. For instance, if your tire diameter changes, a new ratio can be calculated to give exactly the same MPH result. It is interesting to note that a change in tire diameter of 0.100" is equivalent to more than 1 MPH.

To help with this exercise we have created a chart in the Appendix based on our Swedetech CR125 moto engine. We have created an Excel spreadsheet using this formula, which can be downloaded from our website. We have also created a number of different ratio charts for quick reference.

Key Components

Front Gear

Notice the small grooves for the spline.

The front sprocket, or drive gear mounts to the drive shaft on the engine. These sprockets are stamped and machined from steel with small grooves that match up with the shaft. This gear needs to be tight and secure on the shaft to avoid any sloppiness that could damage the drive shaft.

The most common range of sizes for the front drive gears is from a low of 14 teeth to a high of 19 teeth. Changing the drive gear on a shifter is very straightforward. Most engines use a circlip or require the removal of one large nut, as is the case with the YZ 125, or two small bolts as in the CR80. In the case of the large nut, many manufacturers use fold over safety washers, while others use large cup-shaped washers called spring washers.

If you are removing a front sprocket that uses bolts, try to loosen them before you remove the chain and engine. Have someone hold onto the brake, which will keep the gear from turning while you loosen the bolts.

Rear Gear

Split rear gear with key lock.

The rear or axle gear can be made from steel or aluminum. Although steel gears have better wear characteristics, the light weight of the aluminum gears is advantageous in turning the axle. If you use a chain that is in good shape and keep the gears aligned properly, you will have no problem with the aluminum gears wearing prematurely.

Most rear gears are split gears, meaning they come in two halves that are joined together with bolts. This makes it quick and easy to change gears between sessions. One half will have a key way cut into it. The height of the key way is critical. If the key does not fit the key way it can work itself up into the slot on the gear allowing the gear to spin on the axle. Make sure that the key is in good shape and fits properly into the key way or locating holes. Some split gears, like those from RLV, use a small set screw to secure the axle key. This set screw can be tightened to hold the key firmly in the key way.

Gear Alignment

To change the rear gears, loosen the engine mount bolts and pull the engine back a couple of inches. Loosen both sides and then remove the bolts. Remove each half of the gear. Clean the area where the gear was sitting with contact cleaner while it is off. Check that the key way is in good shape. Place the new gear on the axle and install the bolts. Make sure you tighten both bolts an equal amount. This should avoid an excessive gap on one side causing a tight spot in the chain.

When fitting new gears or sprockets it is very important that you get the gear properly aligned. Eyeballing may not be good enough and if you are in doubt, a straight edge rule placed on the sides of the gear will give you the proper alignment. Misalignment of front and rear sprockets is a major cause of rapid wear and loss of horsepower. Chains and sprockets should be checked for worn spots, which could indicate misalignment. Misalignment is usually due to not adjusting the rear sprocket carefully.

To check the alignment, put the kart on a stand, spin the rear wheel and watch how the chain travels along the sprockets. The chain should run on the center of the teeth; it should not run to one side or snake from one side to the other.

To ensure that your gears are in line you need to use a straight edge. Place your straight edge along the front gear and along the rear gear, keeping clear of any bolts, nuts or washers. Look for any gaps between the edge and the gear. Move the rear gear to the left or right to bring it into alignment.

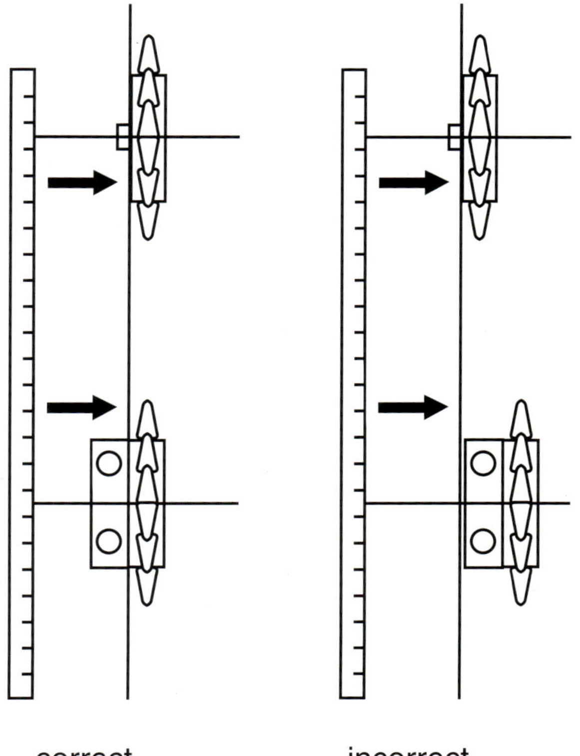

cool trick

Cut a piece of tye wrap and place it in between the key way and the gear. It will squish until the gap is closed and help to prevent the key from loosening and coming out.

Using a straight edge for alignment.

cool trick

Install an axle collar against the gear once it is properly aligned. This way when you change rear gears you know that you are lined up properly.

Master link and chain.

Gearing Tips

Gearing will help you to maintain the proper RPM to keep the engine pulling. This means you must balance your best lap time versus the ability to pass. You must look at each track and decide whether it is a momentum track or a point and shoot track. For a momentum track you are looking for lower RPM that you may hold for a longer period through the corner.

You need to look at your shift points. An improper gear ratio will force you to shift before you exit the corner, which has a negative effect on acceleration and handling. The reason it affects acceleration is that the kart is heavily loaded in the corner. The time spent while you lift for shifting, combined with the heavy load, will slow the kart substantially more than shifting when the kart has completed the turn. Also, when you lift off the throttle to shift, you will unload the kart, which may cause it to veer off line.

The gear you run in qualifying may not be the gear you run in the race. In qualifying you are looking for that one quick lap and to maximize your acceleration from corner to corner. In a race you are looking to be fast on the straight where most of the passing takes place.

Installing the master link clip.

Chain

The next area to tackle is the chain. The chain is your kart's lifeline. Without it you literally go nowhere. Because of the dynamics of a kart and the pounding that shifters take, a good chain, in good condition is a must.

First, consider why a 428 or 0.5" pitch chain is used in shifter kart racing as opposed to a 520 or 0.625" pitch chain. As an example, the diameter of a 0.625" pitch 20-tooth sprocket with its chain is equivalent to 26 teeth on a gear that uses a 0.5" pitch chain. Therefore, the 0.625" layout has jumped an extra 31%, and as we are looking for close ratio changes this is reason enough for the use of a 0.5" pitch. If you have had problems with a 428 chain, watch out for misalignment, correct chain tension, lack of lubrication and axle movement.

During use a chain will stretch, that is, the pins will wear causing extension of the chain. Assume a 2% maximum allowable extension for non- 'O'-ring chains. Using a chain which has been stretched more than the above maximum allowance, causes the chain to ride up the teeth of the sprocket. This causes damage to the tips of the gear teeth, as the force transmitted by the chain is carried entirely through the top of the tooth, rather than the whole tooth. This results in premature wearing of the gears.

Chains are a consumable item on shifter karts. It is a good idea to carry at least one spare chain. It is cheaper to replace a chain than a set of gears. Also a new chain runs smoother, has less friction and actually consumes less horsepower.

It is important to have a chain guard on your kart. This is an item that may or may not come as part of the kart from your dealer. If your kart is missing a chain guard here is a quick trick to mount one. You will need a two inch strip of plastic about 12 inches long. This needs to be mounted in two places, above the rear sprocket and at the very bottom. The top can usually be secured with an L-bracket bolted to the bearing cassette. On some karts the third rail has a tab welded onto it for the chain guard. Mount the chain guard to this point.

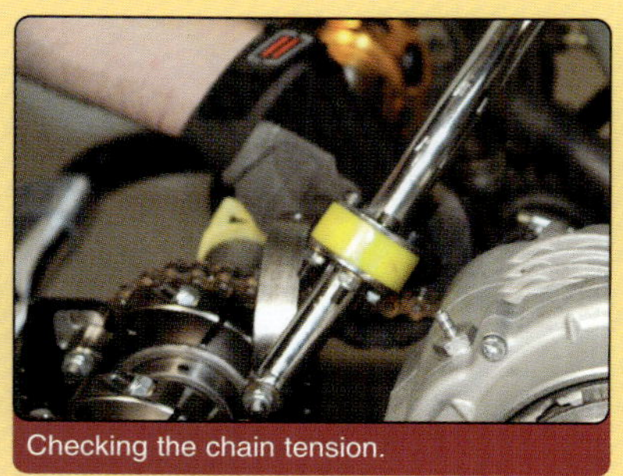
Checking the chain tension.

Chain Length

Having selected the sprockets and gears that you are going to use, it may be necessary to have a number of chains of different lengths. Each one will be suitable for specific ratios as there may not be enough adjustment to cater to all conditions. Add the numbers of teeth on both sprockets together for each ratio. Similar total numbers of teeth require a similar chain length. Here is a quick example of how this works.

Gear Set	Ratio	ChainA	ChainB
14/21	1.500	35	
16/24	1.500		40
19/29	1.526		48
17/26	1.529		43
15/23	1.533	38	

This system is great for keeping your engine in approximately the same position regardless of your gearing combination. This helps to keep the handling consistent and in line with the kart balance. Also, it helps to avoid having to change other components like hoses, sensor leads, fuel lines and mounting brackets.

Put your chains into zip lock bags and write the sizes on the outside and the gear combinations that they fit. This keeps grit from sticking to the chain and also keeps the chain from transferring lube to other parts in your storage box. You can now locate the chain you need quickly and make your gear changes without having to wrestle with other parts of your kart.

With a new chain it is usually necessary to set the proper length to fit your kart. This is done with the help of a chain breaker. A chain breaker allows you to split a chain quickly and efficiently in order to add new links, or remove a few links to modify the chain length. A chain breaker not used properly, can ruin your chain.

A chain breaker is a small block of machined steel with precisely shaped grooves across its surface in which the links of your chain will sit. There are three bolts threaded into the block from the side. By screwing the bolts inward, with an Allen wrench, the ends of the bolts will push into the grooved area. Two of the bolts have a thin end, almost the same diameter as the rollers of the chain. The first bolt has a short end to dislodge the pin and get it started moving. The second bolt has a long end that will push the pin through the link. The third bolt has a flat end that will be used to press the pin back in once the links have been removed.

When you try to push out a roller, it is possible to bend the sidewalls of a link with the thin end of the screw. When you try to connect the chain again, the same is possible if the roller is not properly aligned with the hole in the wall of the link. Be sure that the sidewall is properly aligned to keep this from happening. Once a sidewall of the link is bent, it's unusable and you will have to replace it.

To break the chain, turn the bolt with the narrow end inward; only turn half a turn after the end makes contact with the roller. Then, go back a quarter turn. By letting off the pressure you will ensure that the screw-end and roller have time to align. Be particularly careful at the beginning, when the screw-end needs to find the hole in the link sidewall.

Continue this until the screw-end has cleared the sidewalls of the links and pokes out into the middle of the chain. You can then continue

cool trick

There is a saying in karting that old side pods don't get thrown out, they become chain guards. The plastic from side pods is the ideal thickness to cut and form into a nice chain guard.

Always run with a chain guard.

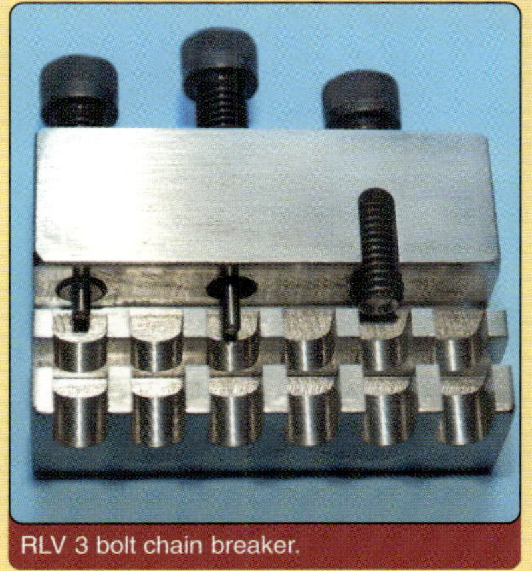

RLV 3 bolt chain breaker.

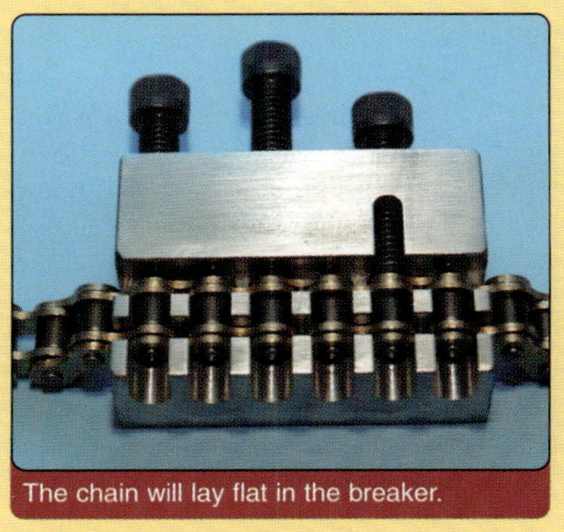

The chain will lay flat in the breaker.

Check tension at the mid point of the gears.

Always use the engine adjustment bolt.

Make sure your engine mount is tight.

without going back a quarter turn. Press the roller out all the way towards the opposite link sidewall. Be careful towards the end, making sure you don't press the roller out too far. Just press it out far enough so that it clears the inner link's sidewall, but still sticks in the wall of the outer link. Pull apart the ends of the chain. Make sure you are removing the proper roller pin. Remember that you have to match up the ends when you put the master link back on.

Next is to add in a piece of chain or re-connect the chain. Place the two chain ends into the groove of the chain breaker, so that the roller, which was pressed out is now pointing towards the end of the flat-ended bolt. You can begin to tighten the bolt until it makes contact with the roller and begins to press it back into the chain.

Again, use the half turn in, quarter turn out method to ensure that the roller and holes align with each other. Be sure to align the holes of the two links that you are connecting. When the end of the roller has reached the sidewalls on the far end, be particularly careful again. Advance the roller in small steps, always letting off pressure in between. Make sure that the outer sidewall does not bend. It may flex a little as the roller is being pressed into the hole, but it should straighten itself again after the roller end is through the hole. The key to success when using a chain breaker is to advance slowly and let off pressure frequently.

Reducing Wear and Tear

There are a number of important steps you can take to ensure your gears and chain not only work well, but also last a long time. Gears should be checked regularly for undue wear. Pointed teeth or stretched teeth are a sign of a worn sprocket. A worn sprocket can rob your engine of power and break under use.

Chain tension is always a good check as you work on the kart. As we outlined in chapter one, the chain needs from 3/8" to 1/2" (9.5 mm to 13 mm) of play. When changing gears or moving the engine, make sure the engine mount is retightened with a minimum of a 3/8" (9.5 mm) of slack at the midway point between the sprockets. Having your chain snap can cause expensive damage to your kart. If your chain is damaged, worn or overstretched, replace it now. When fitting a new chain, ensure that the gears are correctly aligned and the chain and gears are well lubricated.

Make sure the chain guard is in place. This tech item is good protection to you and will keep your kart clean of flying grease. I recommend a high quality chain lube like Torco Power Slide Titanium Series chain lube. Lube the chain before every run. Be neat about this process by placing a rag or paper towel on the frame under the chain. Any lube that flies past the chain will hit the rag and not get on the frame. Try to wipe up any excess chain lube. Remeber to apply chain lube from the inside out, where the chain and the gears meet.

A chain that is dirty can be cleaned. You can soak it in WD40, which will remove the dirt, and also remove the grease in the rollers. This is only a temporary fix for a chain that has been run through the dirt. You will need to heavily lubricate the chain after it is cleaned this way.

Get in the habit of cleaning your gears before you put them away. Put each one in a zip lock bag and mark the size on the outside. This makes finding the one you need quick and easy and keeps your gears from banging into each other in storage.

RACE DAY SET-UP

Race ready with the YOTA

Fast off the trailer

The most important part of racing is prepping your kart before you go to the track. The right preparation will not only help you win races, but will make racing a lot more enjoyable. Make sure you have checked every nut and bolt for tightness and make sure every drill bolt is properly cotter pinned or safety wired. As we discussed in chapter one, this exercise is great for uncovering any potential problems. Before you load up your gear, make sure your kart is race ready. I am a big believer in getting everything done on your kart before going to the track. That way, if you happen to run into any problems along the way, you won't have the added stress of still having to finish prepping your kart at the track.

When you get to the track, get yourself set up and get signed in immediately. Take a couple of minutes to scope out the area to find a good pit spot. I always want to be central to the washrooms and the starting grid. During the race day you will spend a lot of time running between both of these places. Unload your kart onto the kart stand and set up your pit area. A pop-up sunshade tent is a great idea. It keeps the sun off of you and your kart. Think about picking up a 12' x 12' (3.7 m x 3.7 m) piece of outdoor carpet at the local home improvement store. This helps to keep the dirt and dust down in your pit area. Some tracks that pit on asphalt require a covering of some kind to keep spilled fuel or oil off the surface. Set up your tools on the tailgate of your truck or on a work table. For karting, you do not need a lot of tools, so have them ready to go, laid out, as you need them.

Get your pit spot organized.

Organize all of your parts boxes so you can find them quickly and easily. This means not stacking them ten high so you spend your day sorting and searching for parts. Label the outside of each box clearly or try to get different colored lids. Put all of your cleaners in one box, all your spare parts in another, etc. Try to find a pit layout that works for you and stick to it. You need to be able to find things quickly. Have all your charts ready on a clipboard so you can make notes. Fill in your primary chart indicating date, track, weather, event, class and other details. See page 120 in the Appendix for a Race Day Information Sheet. Go to a general all-purpose store, and purchase a cigarette lighter power adapter to run your computer. That way if you get to a track and find they don't have a power outlet, you can run your computer off your car battery.

Get your tools and parts ready.

Next, you should do a quick visual check of all water hoses, fuel lines, fuel filters and cables. Make sure your water and fuel lines are not chaffing on anything. Check that you're getting full throttle. Also, check that your throttle stops are set correctly to keep from stretching or breaking the cable. Make sure that both your clutch and throttle cables slide inside their housings freely. Check to make sure you have a little bit of play in your clutch cable so it won't drag.

The next step is to write down your baseline chassis set-up to make sure you can track your changes throughout the event. This will include settings like the front track width, rear track width, ride height and tire pressures. See page 6 of the Appendix for a Chassis Set-up Chart.

As a quick reminder, or if you do not have any information to work from, here are some quick starting points for your baseline. The idea is to start off so that you have adjustments on either end of the handling

hot tip

If you have a pop-up tent, hang your clipboard right above where the kart will sit. That way it is easy to grab and make notes.

spectrum. For ride height, start with the middle setting. If the kart has only two settings, high and low, choose the lower setting. Front track width should also be set in the middle of the available range. Rear track width should be 54" for 80's and 54.5" for 125's. This is the measurement from the outside of the left rear tire to the outside of the right rear tire.

Set the tire pressures to your HOT settings, then measure and write down the circumference of each tire. In order to keep the corner weights the same, it is usually best to have as close to equal tire circumference as possible. However, if they are off, it's usually best to have the biggest rear tire on the side toward the outside of the track, while the bigger front tire should be mounted on the side closest to the inside of the track. With the stagger set this way, the kart will turn better and scrub less speed for the majority of the corners on the track. As outlined earlier, I recommend 12 psi in the front and 15 psi in the rear for a soft tire, a 15/18-psi combination for a medium compound tire and 20/23-psi for a hard compound tire. These are recommended HOT tire pressures.

Next, plug in your computer and start up the software. One of the things you will need to do while you have the tire circumference reading at HOT pressures is to configure your computer for MPH. Now reset your tire pressure from the HOT pressure settings to the COLD pressure settings. Measure the tire circumference again and make notes on your set-up chart. This usually means that you should start your COLD tire pressures 2 to 3 psi lower than the desired HOT pressures. Remember, the tires on the outside of the track will heat up more than the tires on the inside of the track. For this reason you may find that you need to stagger the side-to-side COLD pressures in order to arrive at the desired HOT pressures.

Make sure the front hub bolts and the rear hub bolts are tight, and check the wheel nuts on all four wheels. Next you should check all your fluid levels, including your brake fluid, radiator coolant and gearbox oil. This is a good time to lube the chain. As we talked about earlier, be deliberate and lube the chain from the inside out. When lubing the chain, more is not necessarily better. The idea is to apply only one coat of lube on the length of the chain. Applying any more than this will only create excess mess and attract more dust.

The next step is to warm up the engine. Put in fuel and prime the fuel system as we discussed in chapter one. Correctly priming the engine is the key to starting your kart on the first try, every time. It's easier to take the time to prime your fuel system correctly, than to waste a lot of time and effort pushing your kart around the pits to fire off. Put the engine in third gear and pull up on the choke. Have someone apply a small amount of throttle as you spin the back tires to fire up the engine. Don't forget the Hot Tip for one-person starting. Once the engine is running, put the gearbox in neutral for moto engines or first gear for ICC engines.

Now, remove the radiator cap and check to see if the water is swirling or flowing past the top of the radiator. If you don't see water moving, then stop the engine immediately. You probably have some air in the system. Burp the air out of the radiator and cooling system as outlined in chapter one. Once you do have water flow, put the cap back on. Let the engine warm up for a couple of minutes. The cylinder and radiator should get warm simultaneously. If only one seems to be getting warm, then shut the engine off and check your cooling system again.

hot tip

The first thing I do after unloading my kart is to set my wheel nut wrench and air gauge in the seat. This reminds me to check both my wheel nuts and air pressures before I go out on the track.

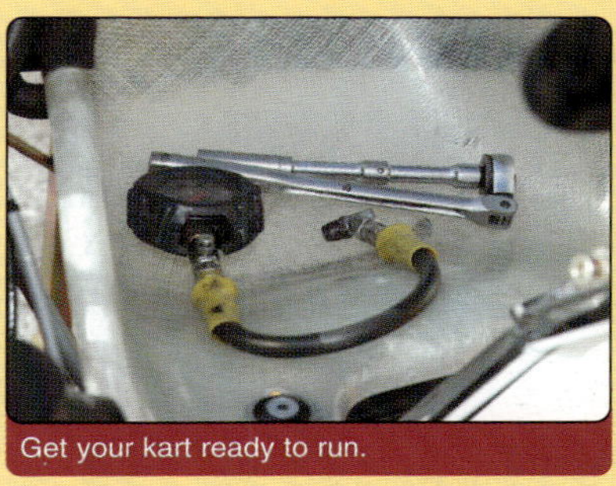

Get your kart ready to run.

Complete your pre-race routine.

cool trick

It is good idea to set up your computer in your truck or trailer. This means you need a long download cord, which is usually available from your data acquisition manufacturer. Doing this will keep the sun off the screen making it easier to read along with helping to keep your lap top computer clean.

warning

Race gasoline is highly flammable. Never refuel in the vicinity of an open flame, or while smoking. Keep all fuels out of the reach of children.

GASOLINE CAN CAUSE INJURY.

Feel the engine come up to temperature.

cool trick

When putting tape on your radiator, make a little tab at the top by folding over three inches at the top end of the tape. This will make it easy to take off while driving on the track should the temperature rise too quickly.

Fold tabs at the top of the tape.

Be prepared to have fun (and win)

Before you head out onto the track, you might want to consider applying tape to the radiator depending on the weather conditions. I use tape vertically lined on my radiator to keep the temperature where I want it. It is important to practice pulling off the tape while you are driving. If I'm waiting on the grid, I will practice reaching over so that I can make a mental note of exactly where the tape tabs are located. You can then begin to remove the strips as the engine temperature rises. Keep an eye on your temperature gauge during practice. Remember, for optimum power and reliability, find out the recommended operating temperature from your engine builder. See page 121 in the Appendix for a Pre-race Check List.

The last thing I do is to locate a spot on the track to place my beacon. The ideal spot is one that I have used from practice sessions so that my data will overlay on top of itself with no differences. It is also very helpful to place the beacon in an area just before the pit in-road. This will keep you from doing an extra "cool down" lap and save you time to use for making changes to your kart. Many times on a race weekend, the operator of the track will take the responsibility of placing a beacon out. If it's more than a one-day event, don't count on the same beacon being out the entire weekend. For this reason, it's important that you know where the beacon is located in case you have to replace it with your own. Make a note of the location of the beacon on your set-up sheet.

Now it's time to suit up and head out onto the track. Make sure all of your driving equipment is in good condition. Clean off your visor with a mild cleaner, using a clean paper towel to avoid scratches. Run your first set of practice laps. The first time out for the day, it is important to take the time to gradually warm up your engine and transmission. The first time out will also set the pattern for your procedures for the rest of the day. Get into the habit of doing certain things. At the end of your run, make sure you get used to coming off the track fast in order to get a good spark plug reading and tire pressure check.

Immediately, even before you take off your helmet, check your tire pressures. Write down the pressures on your set-up chart. Don't stand around talking with the other drivers. Lift your kart back onto the stand and head to your pit to keep from causing a lot of traffic at the scales. It's easier to remove any grease or grime while the kart is still warm, so once back at your pits, get out a rag and do a little cleaning. Download the data from your data acquisition system to your laptop computer. Make any notes as to how the kart handled on your set-up charts.

Keeping your energy level up is easily overlooked at the racetrack. You must take care of yourself as well as your kart. Don't forget to put some fuel in your body. Make sure you take in lots of fluids during the day. This should include things like water and pure juices, not soda or heavy drinks. Try to bring various types of fruit that you can snack on all day long. Avoid the fast food stand. I always take some time between sessions to have a snack and to keep hydrated. A good time to do this is as the engine is cooling down before taking a plug reading.

Try this snack tip. Having quick pre-made snacks at the racetrack is a must to keep your energy levels at their highest. Buy some plain biscuit mix and make them just like the box says. I add a couple of my favorite ingredients. Personally, I like raisins, to give the biscuits a little natural sweetness, and I throw in some cashews to add a little protein to the mix. My other all-time favorite is my famous PB&R sandwich. It's basically a peanut butter and jelly sandwich, minus the jelly and plus raisins. I know both snacks sound a little different but they definitely do the trick. Not only can they be eaten on the run, but they also stand up to the sometimes harsh track environments.

Try to give yourself time to relax and prepare for the race. Work out a schedule for the day, so you know how much time you have and what you can do to get ready. If possible, try not to work with your race suit on. Putting your suit on and getting ready to race should be a constant routine that helps you to get focused and ready to win.

As the engine cools, this is a good time to have a look around the kart and check for problem areas like hoses chaffing or nuts and bolts loosening from your kart. If your kart is prepared properly, rarely should something loosen or fall off. Pay close attention to the spindle bearing and brake/axle condition on a regular basis. Grab the front wheels and lift them up and down to check if the front spindles have any slop in them. Look at the rear rotor and make sure it is still centered, which indicates that the axle hasn't moved. It's easy to lose a lot of time if the rotor is dragging on the brake pads.

Once the engine has cooled, it's time to do a plug check to give you an idea of how the carburetor jetting is set. Remember, after removing the spark plug, put a piece of clean cloth in the plug hole. This will keep any dirt from getting into the combustion chamber. Plugging the hole will also keep the cold air from rushing in and cooling the cylinder to quickly. For longer engine life, it is better that the piston and the cylinder cool down gradually.

After removing the plug, use the burn chart provided to decide if you want to make a jet change. Even if reading the plug is too advanced for you, I still recommend that you get in the habit of looking at it. By looking at it enough and comparing that with how the engine is running, eventually you will start to see what a good burning plug looks like.

Basic reading of the plug is as follows. You want a nice dark black color around the outer ring looking into the bottom of the plug. That area of the plug will give you an idea of your pilot and low-end jets, which affect the torque and initial throttle response of the engine. If it's a lighter color, you may consider going richer on the jet while the opposite is true if it's too dark. The other area of the plug to read is the inner porcelain (or white part), which is affected by the main jet. The inner porcelain color to shoot for is light tan. Because the main jet controls high RPM operation, going too lean may easily seize your engine.

It is usually better to be on the safe side, or a little dark in color. Although I tend to read the plug right away, I may not actually make a jetting change until just before I go out again. If there is a lot of time in between sessions, the weather may change, which will affect the size of jet that I decide to put in.

Finally, you should check for cracks in high stress areas like your seat and engine mount. Check the engine mount bolts, chain tension and wheel nuts. After lubbing the chain, you should be ready to go out for your next session.

Always check air pressures HOT.

cool trick

After you come off the track, hang your suit under your tent in the shade so it can air out. It helps keep your suit clean and helps to keep you dry. Try to bring a couple of t-shirts and socks to change into throughout the day.

Check your spark plug often.

Place a clean cloth in the plughole.

Look for the proper color.

Changes and Adjustments

Before we make any changes, let's review what we are expecting the kart to do as we enter a turn. As we begin to release the brakes and turn the wheel, the inside rear tire needs to lift just slightly off the ground. This is to get the solid axle to act like a differential so that the kart will be able to turn. Remember, this is achieved by the weight jacking characteristics of the front-end geometry and the cornering forces acting on the weight of the kart and your body.

The effects of our braking, combined with the friction of the tires gripping the track will then continue to further slow the kart. Just before the apex, the kart is at its slowest point and the rear wheel will begin to settle back down on the track. It's at this time that we are able to start rolling on the throttle. Partly because, as we pass the apex and begin to release the steering wheel, balance returns to all four wheels and we are picking up traction. With all of this in mind we can understand where handling problems can arise.

I recommend that you first look at the basics when you are thinking of handling changes. We can ask ourselves things like: Is the front-end slow turning in (push) or too quick (loose)? Did the rear tire lift at all or too much? Does the front-end jacking too much weight, or not enough, cause this? Is the kart transition from turning at the apex to accelerating down the straight smooth and easy to drive? When did the rear tire feel like it began to settle down? Is the kart hopping?

Adjusting front track width.

Understeer

Understeer, also referred to as push, is most often seen as poor corner turn-in. The main cause of understeer is that the inside rear tire is not picking up and the kart has to struggle to turn. If this is the problem, let's talk about how to make it better. We know that anything that we do to increase the weight jacking effect will help lift up that inside rear tire. The most common change is increasing the caster, which will increase weight jacking.

The other change you may not hear a lot about is camber. One way that camber affects understeer is through the size of the contact patch. At most tracks you will see plenty of front tires with substantial wear on the inside edge, yet virtually no wear on the outside. This is due to the camber settings asking only a small part of the tire to do any work. As a result, this smaller tire footprint will have a tendency to overheat, especially in hot conditions. This contributes to premature tire wear and understeer.

The other way that camber affects understeer is that it has the ability to jack weight. It is common for most karts to come with zero camber. Because the profile of a front tire is generally flat across the top, zero camber is a good trade-off between contact patch and weight jacking. The more positive camber you induce, the more the outside edge of the tire pushes down in turning and the more weight jacking you have.

Checking rear track width.

There are many misconceptions about camber on go-karts. It is very common to see racecars using negative camber or the tops of the tires lying inward. Why would this work on a car when the opposite is true on a kart tire? In cars, negative camber is used for a couple of reasons. For one, radial tires on racecars have a more flexible sidewall that distorts considerably under cornering loads. Negative camber helps to overcome this distortion of the tire and keeps the contact patch as big as possible. However, the main reason and the key factor that distinguishes a racecar from a go-kart is the differential. A racecar has one, a go-kart doesn't. Understand this and you understand the key to a go-kart. Most karts are built with adjustable positions or pills that change the angle of both the caster and camber. It is best to check with your frame manufacturer to see the range or procedure that you have to work.

The other change that will affect weight jacking and push is the front track width. Try putting your kart on a stand and turning the wheels. Notice that the outside wheel drops down. Making the front end wider will move it further from the pivot point. In other words, the wider the front end, the more the tire will drop, and the more weight jacking affect.

The other area to help with push, picking up the inside rear tire, is changing the center of gravity. This can be done in many ways. The one that first comes to mind is raising the seat up or tilting it forward. Either of these will raise the weight, which gives the cornering forces more leverage to pick up the tire. Other options to accomplish similar characteristics include, moving your lead up or raising the rear ride height.

And finally, another option is to narrow the rear track width. As discussed in chapter four, imagine a triangle using the driver's head and both rear tires as points of intersection. The narrower you make the rear tires, the steeper you make the sides of the triangle. The steeper the triangle, the higher the center of gravity and the more the kart tends to pick up. So, what happens if you go too far with these changes?

Michael Valiante adjusts brake bias.

Oversteer

The most common cause of oversteer is the kart jacking too much weight. When this happens the inside rear tire picks up too much, which makes the front end darty and the kart loose. The other clue that this may be happening is if you have excessive hop during turn in. Turn in hop is created from the inside rear tire picking up and slamming back down hard.

How do you fix this problem? It's really just the opposite of what we just talked about. To make the kart jack less weight, you want to reduce the front-end geometry. Things like less caster, less positive camber, and narrower front wheel width, will fix a kart that is darty and/or loose. Changes for less hop can include lowering the seat, moving down your lead, dropping the rear ride height, or widening the rear tire width.

TJ Ross gets a little loose on exit.

Extra Frame Rails and Torsion Bars

Most modern karts come with removable frame rails and torsion bars. The effects of bolt on frame rails and torsion bars seem to confuse many people. As with any other change, having an understanding of what the problem is, and understanding how the change may affect it, is the key. Let's start with the basics.

The effect of adding frame rails or torsion bars is pretty straightforward; they stiffen the kart. Which kart jacks more weight, a stiff or soft kart? A stiffer kart jacks more weight because the frame absorbs less of the twist. If going stiff with the frame helps with weight jacking, resulting in more front-end grip in the rain, when does it hurt?

The answer is when traction suffers. Going too stiff on the frame will make the rear end not as compliant to the track or over the bumps.

Jake Pierson with a little oversteer.

Making a jetting change.

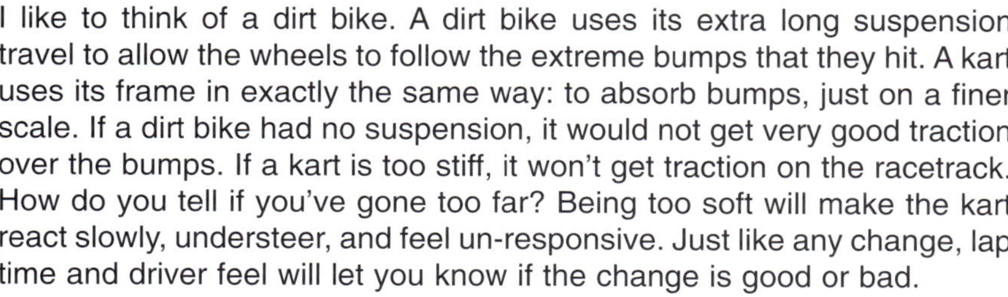

I like to think of a dirt bike. A dirt bike uses its extra long suspension travel to allow the wheels to follow the extreme bumps that they hit. A kart uses its frame in exactly the same way: to absorb bumps, just on a finer scale. If a dirt bike had no suspension, it would not get very good traction over the bumps. If a kart is too stiff, it won't get traction on the racetrack. How do you tell if you've gone too far? Being too soft will make the kart react slowly, understeer, and feel un-responsive. Just like any change, lap time and driver feel will let you know if the change is good or bad.

Hubs and Axles

Hubs and axles act in a similar way when it comes to being too stiff or too soft. Generally speaking, you want them to be as stiff as possible without sacrificing traction. As soon as the tire is not able to follow the bumps you will lose grip and slow down. An axle has more of an effect than the hubs because the axle affects a much longer area. If you get to a point where you run out of range with the hubs, changing the axle is the next step. Again, it's all about trial and error: seeing what is fast for you.

Seat Struts

Seat struts are designed to basically stiffen or soften the rear of the kart, specifically the seat area. Because seat struts are attached to the top of the seat they have a big effect on picking up the rear wheel and also a big influence on traction off the turn. Usually, if the kart is understeering excessively, adding seat struts will help the kart to pick up the rear wheel and turn the kart. Going too far, or adding too many struts, will make the kart not compliant over the bumps. You want to load the tire as much as possible with the number of seat struts, without hurting traction. When you apply the throttle, you shift the weight of the kart back, to the rear wheels. You need just the right amount of flex or "suspension" from the struts to gradually load the rear tires. Loading the tire too hard or too fast will result in a loss of traction.

Alignment

When trying to diagnose handling problems, it is very important to make sure the problem is not the front-end alignment. Anytime you make a caster or camber change, it is recommended that you re-check the toe settings. Toe in can easily contribute to poor turn in as it makes the kart more resistant to changing directions by lessening weight transfer.

Having excessive toe in can make for a darty front end on turn in, while too much toe out can cause excessive front tire wear. The toe should be set at 1/16th to 1/8th toe out on the stand. Remember, when the kart is put on the ground and the driver steps in, the flex of the chassis will bring the toe alignment closer to zero.

Worn steering components can cause substantial negative effects on handling. Worn components contribute to unstable alignment settings in transitional stages of the corner. It doesn't take very much wear in the tie rod ends, kingpin bearings or wheel bearings to affect alignment and weight jacking. Make sure all the front-end components are in good condition and replace them as required before you attempt to make handling changes.

Lube the change before each session.

Tires

Tires are the point of contact between the kart and the track. Because of this, tires are the single most important part of the shifter kart in relation to grip. The best chassis in the world is only able to grip and handle to the capacity of the tires. If the tires are old and hard, chassis adjustments may seem extreme to compensate for the bad rubber. This surprises a lot of drivers because they tune on old tires and come race day switch to new rubber. All of a sudden, the kart goes from unresponsive and pushing, to loose and too darty. Make sure you always note the condition of your tires on your set-up sheet before making handling changes.

Brake Maintenance

Properly working brakes are important for many reasons. Brake performance affects your ability or inability to pass people and to be consistent while driving. If overlooked, brakes also can have a negative effect on straight-line speed by excessively dragging on the rotor. For these reasons, you should take the time to maintain your brakes and check for any problem areas. Some of the basic checks are making sure that the pads are not worn too much and that your rotors are centered. It's also important to check the travel of the pedal. Make sure the brake rods are not obstructed for any reason and that your pedal comes back far enough to release the brakes completely.

Cleaning

Again, start with a dry rag and remove as much dust and grime as possible. Clean in and around the rotor hub and the caliper themselves. Take brake cleaner and use the little nozzle to spray into the caliper, being careful not to overly soak the brake pad. It is important that you use safety glasses to protect your eyes from flying brake cleaner. Cover any painted parts to make sure the surface is not marked. Immediately after spraying with brake cleaner, use compressed air to dry and clean the surface.

Changing brake pads and shimming

At some point you will have to change your brake pads. Most pads are held in place by a long pin or bolt. In most cases, you should be able to change the pads without having to remove the calipers. Many kart brakes require shims to keep from having excessive pedal travel. Excess pedal travel costs you time on the track. As you might imagine, it takes more time to go from gas to brake. This means you will be coasting more. If your brakes use shims, keep in mind that you want the pads as close as possible without dragging. If you have a self-adjusting brake similar to the Brembo units, no shimming is required.

Bleeding

I recommend that you bleed your brakes after every race or three days of practice. First, find out what the recommended fluid is for your caliper. Not all brake fluids work the same. Putting the wrong grade of fluid in the brake system will swell the seals and cause major problems for you on the track.

To bleed brakes, first top up the fluid in the master cylinder. Please note, brake fluid is made with ingredients that attract moisture

125cc karts have two master cylinders.

hot tip

If you have a lot excessive dust build up on your brakes, use an old toothbrush and the brake cleaner to scrub the surfaces clean.

warning

Always wear safety glasses when working with brake fluid. If you accidentally get brake fluid into your eyes, it can cause serious injury. **See a doctor immediately.**

Rear calipers are bigger in size a power.

cool trick

When bleeding brakes, cut a small piece of clear 1/4" tubing and slip one end over the brake nipple, and put the other end into a small container. This way you can control where the fluid goes.

Check the brake rotor bolts often.

cool trick

For a guaranteed way to remember your beacon, take an 8.5" by 11" piece of paper and fold it in half. Write beacon on it in big/bold letters and slip in front of the speedometer every time you stick your beacon out on the track. Now, at the end of the day that piece of paper will remind you to pick up your beacon.

from the air. Keep the brake fluid container sealed and put the top back on the master cylinder as soon as possible. Also, brake fluid contaminates many surfaces; make sure you wipe up any spilled fluid immediately.

Now, have someone slowly pump the pedal a few times and then hold pressure. Loosen the bleed screw and watch for fluid and possibly air bubbles to flow out. Tighten the bleed screw and then instruct your helper to let off the brake pedal. Communication between you and your helper is the key to successful brake bleeding. If your helper lets off the brake pedal with the bleed screw still open, you will suck air back into the caliper and have to start the process over from the first step. If you happen to spill fluid on the caliper, remove it with brake cleaner. Repeat as required until you remove all of the air and the pedal feels hard. Keep checking the fluid level as you move from brake to brake. Brake fluid cannot be recycled or reused. Once it has run through the system it is contaminated.

Kart Preparation

Before I load up to go home, I make mental notes of areas that I can improve on for the next time out. These may range from kart preparation, to ideas learned from handling, to the simplest of things like a pit spot. However, it's important that you go over these improvements, while they are still fresh in your mind. Take the time to make all of your final notes and complete all of the charts. File these by track and event so you can go back to them the next time out.

Before transporting my kart, I do a couple of basic things to it. Drain all the fuel out of the fuel tank and carburetor. It is much easier on the O-rings and gaskets to not be submersed in fuel for the week or so until you go out again. Take the time to wipe the grease off your kart while it's still fresh. This will also give you a chance to visually check for any parts that may have broken and need replacing.

cool trick

Old tires make great supports to put under your kart for transport. Place them under the chassis to provide a nice cushion that will keep the wheels off the floor.

WET WEATHER SET-UP

Be ready to race in the rain.

The great equalizer

Rain has been called the great equalizer, and for good reason. Racing in the rain reduces the influence of big horsepower and the latest features of the newest chassis. What becomes important is how well you set up your kart and drive it in extremely slippery conditions.

Another big factor with rain set-up is that the conditions are always changing. The track may go from being wet with the sun out, to quickly drying in patches in just a few laps. As people in the mid west like to say, "If you don't like the weather, just wait 10 minutes." How much you change your chassis set-up or driving style will depend on how quickly the weather is changing, for better or worse.

If you want to get an unfair advantage in the rain, just be prepared. Most racers do not spend enough time preparing for foul weather. There are a number of unique components and specific changes that need to be made to your kart to race in the rain. How important is learning to drive in the rain? Michael Schumacher grew up with a family go-kart track. The only time he was able to use the track was when there were no customers, which usually meant it was raining. That may be one reason he is one of the best in the world.

Deep grooves to wash away water.

How rain changes everything

Because of the low grip conditions created by the rain, you will never generate the amount of side force normally found in dry conditions. What you will usually encounter in the rain is extreme understeer. This is because it is now very difficult to get the kind of inside rear wheel lift that you need to turn the corner. As we learned earlier, not getting the right amount of rear wheel lift causes the front end to push. Because of the lack of grip, major changes need to be made to the chassis set-up.

The other area that can change in wet weather is our driving technique. In the dry, we drive our ideal line based on the theory of R=MPH. With more or less everybody driving the same line, eventually the track builds up grip as the rubber is laid down. The problem is that the same rubber that helps with grip in the dry, actually hurts grip in the wet. The reason for this is simple, built up rubber does not allow the water to soak into the track. It would have the same effect as laying a rain tarp flat on the ground and then soaking it with water. The tarp would be extremely slippery to walk on because the water has no place to go.

The other reason is that, excess oils, like chain lube, fuel and transmission oil, collect on the racing line. We all know the effects of trying to mix oil and water: it's impossible. On the track, the combination of the oils and water makes for an extremely slippery racing line.

Look out for standing water.

Preparation

You will find that many of the components you use for rain conditions do not apply for the dry conditions. For this reason, I have found that having one box or area where you can put your entire rain set up is a great habit. In the case of a sudden rain shower, having everything in one spot will make the changeover to a rain set up much easier and quicker.

Also, watch the weather. In the old days, before weather radar, the Ferrari F1 team would call all the Italian restaurants in the area to see where the weather was and if it was raining or not. This trick helped to keep Ferrari on top of their game. Weather tracking has become far more advanced these days. It can be as easy as watching the local newscasts. What you may pick up from doing this helps you to forecast your own race day weather. If you have access to the Internet, you can also get live satellite feeds that will show precipitation levels in your area. The last thing you can do on race day is to have a radio tuned into the local weather channel.

Tires

Rain tires, as you might imagine, are very different from slicks. Most noticeably, they are made with grooves that are designed to push or pump out the water. For maximum grip, rains are also made from a very soft compound rubber. You would think that this soft rubber would wear out quickly. In wet conditions, the soft rubber is able to last longer because the water on the track cools the rain tires. However, when rain tires do overheat because of drying track conditions, they begin to chunk and will fall apart quite easily.

Just like slick tires, correct air pressure in rain tires is important for lap times. Because of the cool conditions, the COLD to HOT air pressures will not change as much. I would recommend 12-15psi HOT for the front, and 14-18psi HOT in the rear. Remember, it is still important to check your tires HOT, and adjust the COLD pressures accordingly.

Air Box and Cover

There are a number of things to do on your kart to have a trouble free day in the rain. The first area to take care of is the air intake. Rain tires kick up a fine mist of water and grit from the track surface. If this is sucked into the carburetor, your engine will misfire. Suck enough water into the engine and you're looking at a possible piston seizure or, at the very least, excessive engine wear.

So, to protect your engine from the elements, you need to replace your high flow, gauze style air filter with an air box and rain hood. The air box and rain hood are best positioned, in an area so that the mist won't get in. This usually means facing backwards, toward an area of clean air. Because of the extra weight of the air box, it is important that a mounting bracket be used to secure it. Supporting the air box will stop it from bouncing excessively and coming off the carburetor.

I also recommend that an internal air filter be used in the air box to ensure that grit does not get into the engine. It is important that you constantly clean the air filter and air box in between sessions to keep them from plugging up.

Electronics

Wet weather will also pose some potential problems with your electronics. The reason is simple; water conducts electricity. Having your electronics in an area that gets wet, may allow the water to short out the electrical system. If this happens you are bound to get a misfire.

The best solution is to have all your electronics mounted in a dry place. Various sized electronic boxes can be purchased at an electronics store that will house your ignition box, sealing it up watertight. Keep the coil dry and seal up any areas susceptible to water seepage, such as

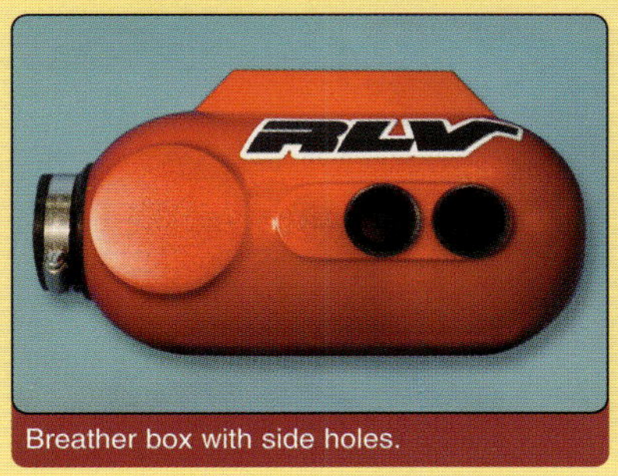

Breather box with side holes.

Breather box with front holes.

Screens keep grit and grime out.

hot tip

In restricting the air opening to keep water and grit out of the engine, you will also be restricting the volume of air that can flow into the carburetor. This will push the fuel/air mixture to the rich side. A jetting change may be in required when you put the air box on.

hot tip

WD40 is an excellent product to repel water from electronics. The first two letters in its name actually stand for water displacement. I spray a liberal amount on all the electronics of my kart whenever driving in wet conditions. If any water happens to get past my sealing efforts, the WD40 will help to displace it before any problems occur.

where the spark lead is attached. Make sure you have a good watertight spark plug boot.

For the data acquisition system, similar steps should be taken to prevent potential problems caused by wet weather. The most fragile components are the dash and the logging unit. The dash is very susceptible to water because it is located on the steering wheel, which places it in the path of water and rain. I've found that you can take a clear sandwich bag and tye wrap it over the dash. It keeps the water out, yet the numbers still remain visible to the driver on the track.

The logging unit is somewhat better protected from the elements due to its location under the front fairing. However, shielding it from any water that may get splashed on it will help to keep it protected. Again, using a plastic bag is a great way to seal it from water.

Driver

There is no quicker way to spoil a perfectly good day of driving in the rain than by becoming cold and wet. It's not just that it will make you uncomfortable, getting cold will have the effect of tightening your muscles, which will slow your reflexes and reaction times. To be fast in the rain you have to have lightening quick reflexes.

A good rain suit is a worthwhile investment. You want something that is of good enough quality to be fully water repellent, but not too heavy that it will restrict your movement. I would recommend buying a two-piece suit so that you have the option of just using half if the conditions begin to dry. If you are heading to the track and forgot your rain suit, most general merchandise stores carry rain suits that will get you by for the day. Also, having an extra change of socks, t-shirt and underwear to keep warm and dry will come in handy in wet conditions.

Rain gear is required to keep dry.

Hands and feet are a little harder to keep dry. You can buy slip-on rubber coverings that do a good job of keeping your feet dry. However, they are definitely a little cumbersome. The other solution is to have an extra pair of driving shoes and always start with a dry pair. You can also purchase a boot dryer from a local shoe store. This unit does an excellent job of drying off your shoes in between sessions. However, it will require you to have a power outlet.

As far as keeping your hands dry, I have not really found anything that does a great job at keeping water out. You can purchase watercraft or wetsuit gloves that, although not waterproof, do keep wet hands warm. The only drawback to these types of gloves is that they are not abrasion resistant, a requirement for karting safety.

I think the best plan of attack is to have a couple of pairs of gloves with you at the track and to dry them in between sessions. If you do not have a heater, start your car and use the dash heater to dry your gloves. Kart races are usually short enough that if you start with a pair of warm and dry gloves, your hands will stay warm until the end of the race.

hot tip

Drill a couple of 1/4" holes in the lowest part of the seat on either side. The small holes won't affect the integrity of the seat and will allow the water to drain from the seat and help to keep your butt dry.

Helmet preparation is very important to your visibility on the track. If you can't see, you're not going to be able to drive very well. The first area on a helmet that needs to be addressed are the air vents. Any water that makes its way into the helmet through these vents will fog your visor. Vents on the top or sides of the helmet should be taped to prevent water from working its way inside.

As far as the shield itself, many helmet manufacturers make an "anti-fog" visor, that is designed with a special coating or layer that prevents fogging. These usually do a great job, as long as the shield is relatively new. Special care should be taken when cleaning this style of visor, as it is easy to scratch or rub off the fog coating. Also, you can buy a number of different anti-fog solutions or coatings that you can apply to your existing shield. These are available from racing performance shops or your local ski shop.

The last area is to make sure your shield seals around the helmet to prevent water seepage. This is accomplished with the foam or rubber liner that runs around the outside of the eye port. If this is torn or missing, it would be a good idea to replace it. You can usually purchase new liner strips from your helmet manufacturer.

Baseline Setup

As we described before, the problem we deal with in wet weather conditions is the lack of grip. The first handling problem we will face in the wet is the kart laying too flat on the track and developing massive understeer. If you think back, the inside rear tire must pick up in order to act like a differential and allow the kart to turn. So, the question is, what kind of changes do we make so that the kart jacks more weight or has a higher center of gravity. The other area we will look at is rear traction. How soon and how hard you can get back to the throttle will have a big effect on lap times. We will look at the changes you can make to increase rear traction.

Front-End

Starting with the front-end, you can begin by adding more caster and more positive camber. Also, widening the front track will jack more weight and help the front-end to get more grip. Lowering the front ride height will also help by adding more rake into the kart and adding more front corner weight. Lowering the front end means taking washers from the top of the spindle and moving them to the bottom.

Front Toe

Going as far as 3/8" to 1/2" (9.5 mm to 13 mm) toe out is not uncommon for a rain set-up. Adding toe out heats up the inside of the tire, which helps with grip. Adding toe out also increases the Ackerman of the inside front tire in the corner. This extra Ackerman on the front inside tire actually helps to drag the front-end around the corner. The reason that this extreme toe out is acceptable in the wet is because the track surface is slippery and cool, keeping the tire temperatures in an acceptable range.

Rear End

To combat understeer, we are looking for things that will help pick up the inside tire, such as center of gravity, track width and ride height. Lifting up or tilting your seat forward will raise the center of gravity. Re-locating your lead to the top of the seat will also help to raise the center of gravity.

Narrowing your rear track will also help the kart pick up the inside rear wheel, by making the difference between the two radiuses of the two rear wheels smaller. In the rain, don't be surprised if you end up moving the wheels in a couple of inches per side. This may require the use of special rain hubs with removable hub stops to achieve this narrower

hot tip

To stop your sheild from fogging, grab a bottle of liquid dishwashing detergent and put a small amount on a towel. Apply to the inside of your shield, then take another clean towel and wipe off the soap until the shield is dry. If done properly, this little bit of soap residue left on your shield will keep the visor fog-free.

cool trick

Part of what makes your visor fog up is the warmth of your breath hitting the cold surface of the visor. Run a piece of tape across the opening over the bridge of your nose. This will keep your breath from rising up inside your helmet.

cool trick

For a quick toe change when time is tight, loosen the rod end jam nuts and turn each rod one turn. It may not be exact, but it will help in a pinch. Do not forget to re-adjust the front alignment of the kart when racing goes back to a dry track.

cool trick

If you want a quick way to change your center of gravity, pre-cut a couple of 1" pieces of rubberized foam that fit in the bottom of your seat. Now you can quickly move your weight up if you don't have a lot of time.

Try to work under a tent or roof.

Kart control is very important.

Run off the racing line.

width. Finally, raising your rear ride height will add more rake to the kart and will raise the center of gravity.

A note of caution; you can go too far! Just like with a dry set-up, jacking too much weight, or picking up the inside rear tire too much, will result in its own set of handling problems. If you go too far, your kart will become very darty and hard to drive. You may also start to feel excessive hop. These conditions will make trying to be smooth in the rain, very difficult.

Extra Frame Rails and Torsion Bars

Frame rails and torsion bars have a similar effect in the wet as they do in the dry. That is, bolting them in or out will stiffen or soften the kart. The question is, do we want a stiffer kart or softer kart for the rain. Remember a stiffer kart will jack more weight and help with front grip on a slippery track. So, if your kart is under steering you might want to try adding frame rails or torsion bars. The downside to this is that going too stiff may hurt traction. In bumpy or slippery conditions you need the frame to be compliant so that you aren't overloading the rear tires. The thing to keep in mind is that there is no set change that will guarantee to make you faster. Success will come from understanding the conditions you are in, having an idea of what you are trying to do and then experimenting by trial and error.

Hubs and Axles

Hubs and axles have the majority of their effect onr traction. Some people think that when it rains you want the shortest hub and the softest axle. That's just not always the case. Again, you want the to load the tire as hard as possible without sacrificing grip. If you too stiff for the track the tires won't be compliant enough to follow the road and you'll lose traction. Conversely, if you're to soft and not loading the tire hard enough, you will also be giving up grip.

Seat Struts

Just like in the dry, seat struts have a big effect on picking up the inside wheel and traction off the corner. Just like other changes, there is no right or wrong way to go. Try to figure out what your kart is doing and then make a change. First try adding seat struts. Does the kart turn better because the inside rear wheel is picking up more? Did the rear of the kart lose a little traction on acceleration? Now try with the struts disconnected and feel the affects. The thing to remember in the rain with all changes is that you will probably never get a perfectly balanced kart. The goal is to see which change gives you the quickest lap time with your driving style.

Gearing

Because of the wet conditions, you will generally see a slower top speed down the straightaway. This is for the simple reason that your corner speed leading onto the straight will be lower, and you have to brake earlier for the corner after the straight. It is sometimes suggested that you want a taller gear for the rain. I disagree. Even though a taller gear will help to control wheel spin in the corners, it will also take away the power you have.

I would rather learn to control wheel spin with my throttle foot and have all the power available for me to use down the straight. So, as far as actually choosing the gearing, it's really the same as how we do it in dry conditions. That is, get the best compromise for the maximum speed down the straight and the best pull out of the corners.

Brakes

The last thing that needs to be changed is the brake bias. On a 125cc shifter kart with front brakes you will want to add brake bias to the rear. The reason is really simple; on a dry track you have more grip and are able to brake harder. When you brake harder, you transfer more weight to the front, and in turn need more front brake pressure. In the wet, if you leave the same brake bias setting, you will tend to lock up the front wheels. I would start by adding two turns of rear brake on the brake bias adjustor for wet conditions.

Driving in the rain

The last area that we will discuss is wet weather driving techniques. By now you should have a good understanding of the dry line theories we discussed in chapter two. Have you ever heard somebody say, "In the wet, stay off the racing line." As we mentioned earlier, the combination of rubber buildup and oils collected on the track make for an extremely slippery racing line. Because of these slick conditions, we have to modify our line in order to get the most grip for braking, turning, and accelerating. How do we do this?

The easiest way to think about this is in wet conditions, drive the track in a completely opposite line from wherever you drive in dry conditions. As extreme as it may sound, this is really a good place to start. So, if you brake on the left side of the track, brake on the right. If you apex on the inside of the turn in the dry, try to apex on the outside of the turn in the wet. If you exit on the outside, try exiting on the inside. In effect, what we are doing is crisscrossing the racing line.

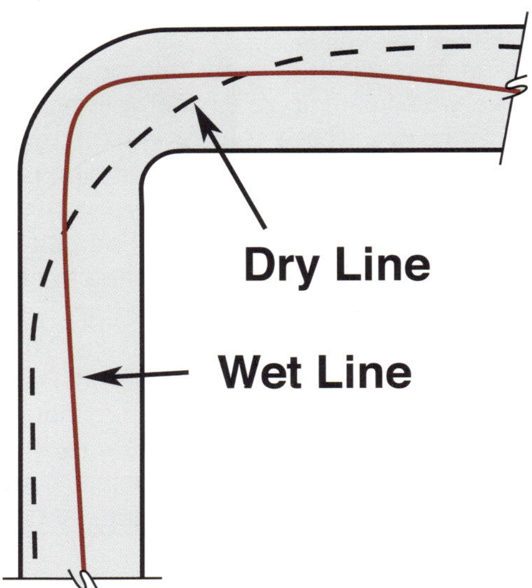

Bridgestone front and rear rain tires.

cool trick

Almost all rain tires have a considerably smaller rear tire circumference, which will affect the gearing in a big way. I've found many times that just changing to the smaller rear rain tires will sufficiently lower the gear to compensate for the slower speed.

Rain tires are narrower than slicks.

Rain tires are shorter than slicks.

Keep an eye on a drying track.

cool trick

In the rain you may want to soften the throttle response, by adding a spring to the gas pedal or make one of the springs heavier. This will help to control wheel spin and loss of traction from getting on the gas too hard.

Be aggressively patient.

warning

Obey all severe weather warnings and apply common sense to all conditions.

Now, how much you avoid the dry racing line really depends on how slippery that line is in the wet. If it's not too slick, you just need to change your line a little. If it's extremely slick, you need to change your line a lot.

Dealing With A Drying Track

Dealing with changing track conditions is very challenging. If you are driving a full wet line and the track starts to dry, your line will change. Slowly you will find yourself inching back toward the dry racing line. How do you know if you have moved back to the racing line too quickly? For one, the amount of understeer will increase dramatically and your lap time will get slower. Getting back on the dry line too soon will also make traction a problem. You will have to fight more to put the power down.

Dealing with a wet or drying track is a lot about experimenting. You need to be constantly moving your line, inches at a time, to test the grip levels of different areas. The mistake that most drivers make is that they make big line changes when searching for grip. By moving your kart around that much, you may go from decent grip to no grip and find yourself spinning off the track.

Chassis set-up is another area that will change. You will find that as the grip level comes back, the kart will become very pointy and hard to drive. You need to slowly begin to change back from your wet set-up, to a dry set-up. It's never going to happen all at once. Even if the track is completely dry, the rain has no doubt washed away most of the rubber. You may find that you will still have some of your wet settings on the kart, like the extra camber or caster, until the grip level builds back up on the track.

Driving Technique

Driving in the rain requires a couple of qualities from a driver that you wouldn't think really go together. I tell drivers to be aggressively patient in the rain. You are dealing with a slick surface that is unforgiving. However, you need to be aggressive and attack the track as if you were in dry conditions. Also, in the wet you will inevitably make some big mistakes and be a little out of control. You need to be aggressive with the kart to recover from these mistakes.

Patience is another virtue of great rain drivers. In the wet, your kart will not handle very well as it fights to deal with braking, turning, and accelerating. Unlike in the dry, where you can get the rear axle to pick up enough to get a good balance, in the wet the handling is usually poor. In the wet, you will come across situations where your kart takes what seems like an eternity to respond to your input. For instance, if the wheel is turned and the kart is still going straight, you need to be patient enough to wait for the front-end to gain grip and actually turn.

The same holds true when accelerating. You are going to constantly fight wheel spin as you work to apply throttle out of the corners. Rolling on the power ever so slowly to keep from spinning the tires takes huge amounts of patience. Some drivers just give up and mash the gas. The problem is that when the wheels are spinning violently, they have exceeded their threshold and have very little grip. And the same holds true when braking for a corner.

Be smooth in the wet.

Look for grip as you run.

Adjust your line as required.

PERSONAL DEVELOPMENT

Back extensions.

Side bends with dumb bells.

Chest press.

Overview

The one thing I've learned about karting, is that getting 80% of the speed required to go fast comes down to practice and learning how to drive. Most people will be able to reach this goal fairly easily. The last 20% is part of what this chapter is about. The ratio of speed gained versus effort exerted for this 20% will seem uneven. That is, you will work a lot harder to get that last couple of tenths than you've ever worked before. However, with the competitive nature of karting, the last two tenths can be the difference between finishing mid-pack or winning.

In the next section we will go into detail on training programs and a diet that I use to prepare for driving. As with anything, it's best to use this as a guideline and then experiment to see what works for you.

Inclined sit-ups.

Weight Training

I like to think of exercise as free time. That is, it's something that any of us can do to improve ourselves as a driver and it's free. The only requirement is motivation and effort. It amazes me how drivers have no problem spending a lot of money on chassis and motor modifications to improve their lap times, but put very little effort into preparing their bodies. What drivers fail to realize is that their body's condition or performance will gain them even more time over the course of a race than any new pipe or motor modification. If, on the last 15 laps of a 25 lap race, you are giving up a couple of tenths per lap because you're tired, the total may add up to a couple of seconds or more. This time loss can be avoided. Here are some basics that I have found to help with driving performance.

As with all physical activity, it's important to be warmed up before attempting an exercise program. That means some light cardio, such as jumping jacks for five minutes, and a little stretching is usually sufficient. Variety with exercise is important to keep from burning out and over-working the same muscles. I have three programs that I set up with similar exercises. The first program is designed for strength.

In strength programs, I will do one warm up set of with approx 15-20 reps with a light weight to loosen up. Then, three more sets with approx 13 reps with a heavy weight to max out. Max out means that you go until you can't physically do another rep. My other program is designed with lighter weights and more reps for endurance training. I still do a warm up set of approximately 20 reps with a very light weight to get loose.

Overhead press.

Forearm curls.

Then, another three sets with 18-20 reps with a medium to heavy weight. A good reference for weight heaviness is that after the 20 reps, you should feel like you are physically able to do another 5-7 reps. The last program is what I call my cruise day. It's designed to give your muscles a rest day while still exerting a little effort to keep from tightening up. You should use extremely light weights and do 20-25 rep sets of approx 50% of your max lifting strength. I vary these three programs by spending most of my time in the strength mode, but then every few days I mix it up with an endurance day or a cruise day.

In a kart, we experience high G-forces that push and pull our bodies in different directions. Just like a tree needs a strong trunk to keep from bending or toppling over in the wind, we also need a strong trunk or midsection to keep our bodies from leaning over in the kart. This is to keep us secure in the kart without relying on holding or bracing the wheel, which affects the handling and consistency of the kart. The first area of our trunk to strengthen is the stomach and back. An excellent lower back exercise is the back extension. As you get stronger you can grasp a flat plate (weight) to your chest to give more resistance. For the stomach, I like to do old-fashioned sit-ups. My favorite is to use an inclined sit-up bench that locks your legs in place. Again, as you get strong, grasping a flat plate (weight) to your chest will add resistance. Abdominal crunches and leg lifts are also great for stomach strength. You can vary the direction of the sit-up by doing a twist at the top, which will strengthen the muscles on the sides of your torso. Another great torso exercise is the side bend.

Working our way up, the next area is the chest, shoulders, and upper back. A few of my favorite exercises are the chest press, the upright row, the shoulder rotation, and the overhead press. I also like the standard biceps curl and the triceps extension. Are you getting arm pump? A great forearm exercise is to take a curling bar with a rope connected to a flat plate. Position your arms over a dead lift curl bar set at chest height. Roll the bar to raise and lower the weight.

The neck is the next group. Extreme caution should be taken whenever exercising the neck as the muscles are easily strained. My favorite exercise is the four way neck machine, which does a great job of exercising your neck in all four directions. If your gym doesn't have this, you can substitute by using a flat plate and a bench. You can lie on all four sides and gently rest a light plate on the side of your head. I fold up a small towel and place it in between the weight and my head to make it more comfortable. Then, just slowly raise and lower your head. Another

hot tip

Many gyms have a few different brand choices of machines that cover the same muscle groups. Every brand of machine works the same muscles in a slightly different way. To really add strength to a specific muscle, vary the brand of machine you use from week to week. The end result will be a muscles that are much stronger.

Side neck machine.

Forward neck machine.

Backward neck extensions.

Forward neck extensions.

warning

Consult your doctor before you begin any exercise program.

one of my favorite exercises for the neck is the shoulder shrug. This can be done using either dumbbells or a barbell.

The legs are a muscle group that many kart drivers overlook because they think they do nothing while driving in a kart. Outside of the obvious throttle and brake application, the goal is to keep them as stable in the kart as possible. My first exercise is the heel raise for the throttle and braking applications. The other two that I like, are the inward and outward leg spread. This exercise is great to strengthen the legs and keep them from spreading excessively out from the gas tank in the corners. I also like to do the leg press, hamstring curl, and the leg extension for general leg fitness.

Shoulder shrugs.

Cardio Vascular Training

The heart and lungs need to be strong when driving. If your lungs aren't strong, an adequate amount of oxygen won't get to your muscles and you'll get tired. My favorite cardio exercise is mountain biking because it is fun and hard. I can put together a number of different rides and easily monitor my progress based on the time it takes to finish a ride. Running is another option and is great because you can do it anywhere. While running is very accessible, the down side is that it's hard on your knee joints. It's always best to run on something other than pavement: either dirt or grass. I am also a big fan of lap swimming. It's a great exercise to increase your lung capacity and strengthen your shoulder area. And finally, the rowing machine is a way to increase the strength of your back and arms while giving you an awesome cardio workout.

Just like with weight training, variety is important to successful cardio training. I like to do easy days, hard days, and for sure a rest day where I do nothing at all. I generally like to do some form of cardio exercise for a minimum of 45 minutes, five times a week. In the case of a bike ride, some of my exercises are a couple of hours in length. It's important that you drink plenty of fluids to keep your muscles working hard. I have found that low sugar drinks, like Cytomax Sport drink, do a great job of keeping you hydrated during a workout.

Calf stretches.

Diet

The next area to address is diet. What you eat is the fuel for your body. Put in poor fuel, and your body will perform poorly. Unfortunately, many people have been raised eating junk foods and breaking those habits is a serious test of willpower. However, just like exercise, you need to decide if winning races and striving for those last few tenths is important to you.

Many people are under the impression that in order for food to be healthy, it's got to taste bad. That's just not the case. It's all about conditioning your body to like the foods that are healthy for you. Over time, you will develop a taste for high-quality food and actually get sick at the thought of eating junk food. I am not a nutritionist; however, I will tell you what has worked for me over the years and what I have learned.

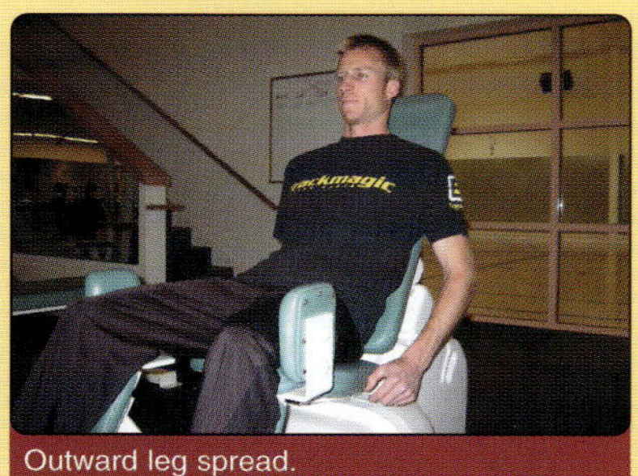
Outward leg spread.

I always try to eat from the four food groups. That is dairy, meat, carbohydrates, and vegetables. I definitely stay away from foods fried with fat or foods that list some type of oil as a main ingredient. Excessive fats in foods are hard to digest. This means your stomach has to work overtime to get fatty foods through your system. That's one reason you will feel so sluggish after eating something big and greasy. Excessive sugars also don't help you with long lasting energy. I stay away from any type of foods that add extreme amounts of sugar. I look for alternatives. In the food industry, so much is labeled as healthy or good for you, but that is not always the case.

Breakfast

Let's start with breakfast. For me, breakfast is essential. It is a chance for me to fill up my "gas tank" and get me off to a good start. I like oatmeal because it is filling and easily digestible. Oatmeal is also full of good carbohydrates that jump start my energy after sleeping for eight hours. In addition, I mix in raisins and cashew nuts. I really like the raisins because they sweeten up the oatmeal and make it naturally sweet. The cashews will give me just enough protein to have solid energy for a couple of hours. If you're not an oatmeal fan, cold cereal works just fine also. Cereals like Cheerios (plain type), Special K, and Corn Flakes work great.

There are a ton of cereals out there to choose from, but most are not very good for you. Brands like Honey Bunches Of Oats, Honey Nut Cheerios, Frosted Flakes, even granola, are all given names to sound healthy, but in reality are loaded with sugar and fat. My advice is to read the labels to check for sugar content and find something that you like. If it's a little bland tasting at first, experiment with things like fruit or some type of nut that you can add to make it taste better. My other breakfast habit is to use rice milk instead of regular milk on cereal. Rice milk is a little easier to digest and allows me to work out harder and sooner. Even though rice milk sounds healthy, you must still read the label and compare the sugars from different brands. If you must have milk, the lower the fat content the better. If you drink whole vitamin D milk now, try 2% for a couple of months and then try skim milk.

Juices and Drinks

Drinks and juices are another area where the labels can many times be misleading. Most juice brands add sugar to sweeten up the taste. It is important to read the labels and find the product that has the least amount of sugar. Soda is another product that has a lot of sugar and should be avoided. If you just have to have a carbonated beverage, try something like Hansens All Natural in a can or Calistoga flavored sparkling water. Probably, the best drink is just plain water. I am always a little skeptical of the cleanliness of tap water, so I buy bottled water. Whenever I'm ordering water in a restaurant, I ask the waiter to bring slices of lemon. Putting a couple of slices of lemon in my glass of water adds a nice flavor.

Snacks

Snacks are essential for me to keep my energy levels up during those times between meals. It's at these times that I don't want to be bogged down by something heavy. I look for instant energy that also lasts a couple of hours. Fruit is always a great supplier of instant energy. I carry around an apple, banana, and orange for those in between meal snacks. As good as fruit is for that quick burst, I also need a snack that stays with me longer. My favorite for this is peanut butter. I make a peanut butter and raisin sandwich because it gives me a great burst of energy from the bread and carbs, but also the protein from the peanuts that I need to sustain the energy for a longer period of time. Peanut butter and jelly is another option. However, because the sugar content of most jellies is

hot tip

Can't get motivated in the cardio department? Try taking a step or kickboxing class at your local gym. It's always motivational to be in a class with other people doing the same as you and having an instructor help with your progress. As a matter of fact, most gyms offer numerous free classes to its members that are fun and a great workout.

Leg extensions.

Hamstring curls.

Bicep curls.

warning

Alcohol and cigarettes will not help you to to be a better athlete or a better driver. If you're serious about driving you shouldn't be drinking alcohol or smoking.

Rowing extensions.

Biking is great cardio exercise.

Motocross is a great work out.

high, I stay away from using it. My other favorite is peanut butter and sliced banana sandwiches. Another great option is trail mix containing nuts and dried fruit. Stay away from the type with chocolate pieces mixed in. Other snacks that seem great, but in reality have a lot of sugar and fat, are the packaged energy bars. Be very leery because even though they say how healthy they are on the packages, most aren't. Read the wrapper and check the ingredients. If sugar and/or some type of oil are predominate ingredients, find something else. If the bar tastes sweet or is covered in something like chocolate, it probably has a lot of sugar.

Lunch

These days it seems that you can't buy a decent lunch anywhere without it being loaded with ingredients that kill your energy. It seems that all the restaurants try to out do one another with the special three-cheese sauce, or the deep-fried something to attract your taste buds. If you eat out, my advice is to go simple. You hardly ever go wrong with a sandwich and a salad. I prefer turkey, chicken or tuna over the roast beef because it's better for you and much easier to digest. However, if it's a tuna or chicken salad sandwich, beware. Many of those mixes are usually full of mayonnaise, which is very high in fat content.

Don't be afraid to ask how they prepare it or even for a sample taste. If it tastes rich and creamy, it's high in fat. The great thing about a turkey sandwich is that you can specify your ingredients or ask for the mayo and mustard on the side and add the amount you want.

My all-time favorite and usual lunchtime order is the chicken burrito. If you stay away from the guacamole and sour cream, the other ingredients are healthy and good. I like to specify black or pinto beans, as refried beans are high in fat. Also, you will usually have a choice of the chicken, grilled or boiled. I will order the boiled variety because it's a lot less greasy. Note---When it comes to healthy Mexican food, I'm talking about authentic Mexican, and not the fast food variety.

Dinner

For dinner, eating out is even more difficult if you are trying to go healthy. The safest bet is usually ordering grilled chicken and a salad. Pasta is also a safe bet as long as it's of the plain variety. Stay away from the entrees with a lot of creamy sauce such as alfredo sauce. Anything that's really creamy is usually made with a lot of fat and butter. Be careful when choosing your sides with your meal. Again, it seems like restaurants continually try to out do each other with unique and unhealthy ingredients in the simplest of things. These days it seems that all you can order is the garlic, fried, something, something, bacon bit, mashed potatoes. If that's all they have, just order a plain baked potato. Fish is also an excellent source of protein and is very healthy. However, if it's breaded or battered it's probably cooked with a lot of butter. The safest bet is to order fish that is grilled or baked. And don't be afraid to ask the waiter how it's prepared. As with any meal, you can usually request that the food be prepared a certain way. That even includes such things as ordering a grilled cheese sandwich at a restaurant. Ask them to grill it without the butter or grease and they usually will have no problem with that. Again, stick with simple foods and you have a better chance of getting something healthy.

Memo's Exercise Program

	Strength programs	Endurance training	Cruise day
Warm Up	warm up set of approx 15-20 reps with a light weight to loosen up.	warm up set of approximately 20 reps with a very light weight to get loose.	warm up set of jumping jacks
Training	three more sets with approx 13 reps with a heavy weight to max out.	three sets with 18-20 reps with a medium weight.	use extremely light weights and do 20-25 rep sets of approx 50% of your max lifting strength.
Stomach and Back			
back extension			
Inclined sit-up bench			
Abdominal crunches			
leg lifts			
side bend			
Other			
Upper Body			
chest press			
upright row			
shoulder rotation			
overhead press			
biceps curl			
triceps extension			
forearm curls			
Other			
Neck			
neck machine			
Neck extensions			
shoulder shrug			
Other			
Legs			
heel raise			
inward leg spread			
outward leg spread			
leg press			
hamstring curl			
leg extension			
Other			

Basic Nut and Bolt Check List*

Date: ______________ Kart: __________________________ Mechanic: ____________________

	✓	Safety Wire	Cotter Pin	Other	Notes
Front End					
King Pin Bolts			YES		
Front Brake Calipers		YES			
Master Cylinders		YES			
Tie Rod Heim Jam Nuts				Left & Right Thread	Tight
Tie Rod End Bolts			YES		
Steering Support Bracket			YES		
Steering Wheel		YES			
Front Hubs or Spindles				Safety Clip	Castellated Nut
Steering Wheel Hub			YES		
Front Brake Rotor Bolts		YES			
Engine					
Ignition and Coil					Snug
Pipe and Silencer				Springs	Cradle
Motor Mount Bolts				Thread Lock	
Carburetor Mounting Bracket				Clamp	Tight
Fuel Pump				Bushing	Snug
Cooling System					
Mounting Brackets				Bushings	Tight
Hose Fittings				Hose Clamps	Tight
Rear End					
Bearing Cassettes (if adjustable)				Thread Lock	Snug
Bearing Set Screws				Thread Lock	Tight
Axle Collars				Clean Surface	Tight
Rear Hubs				Clean Surface	Tight
Rear Brake Caliper		YES			
Rear Brake Rotor Bolts		YES			
Body Work and Bumpers					
Front Bumper					Snug
Rear Bumper				Nylock Nut	Snug
Front Faring Top and Bottom				Rubber Bushings	Snug
Nerf Bar				Nylock Nut	Snug
Side Pods				Nylock Nut	Snug
Floor Pan				Nylock Nut	Snug
Fuel Tank					Snug
Seat					
Right and Left Side Supports				Nylock Nut	Tight
Seat Struts Top Bolt				Nylock Nut	As Required
Seat Strut Bottom Bolt				Nylock Nut	Tight
Front Mounting Tabs				Nylock Nut	Tight

* Example only. Consult your dealer for a detailed maintenance program.

Quick Maintenance Chart*

Date: ____________ Kart: ______________________ Mechanic: __________________

	Pre-Race	After Each Session	After Each Event	Once a month
Front End	Clean	Check	Clean	Re-assemble
Brakes/Rotors/Calipers	Clean	Check Fluid	Replace Fluid	Check Pads
Front Hubs or Spindles	Check Bearings	Adjust	Clean	Re-assemble
Alignment	Check			Adjust
Engine	Remove and Clean	Check	Replace Oil	Top End Rebuild
Ignition and Coil	Check	Check	Inspect	Re-assemble
Pipe and Silencer	Inspect	Check	Clean	Re-assemble
Carburetor	Clean	Adjust	Clean	Inspect
Chain	Adjust	Lube	Inspect	Replace
Cooling System	Check Clamps	Check Level	Inspect	Replace Fluid
Rear Axle	Clean and Inspect	Clean	Remove	Inspect
Bearing and Cassettes	Clean	Check	Clean	Inspect
Set Screws/Axle Collars	Check	Check	Check	Check
Rear Hubs	Clean	Check	Check	Clean
Body Work and Bumpers	Clean	Inspect	Clean	Re-assemble
Seat	Clean	Inspect	Clean	Re-assemble

Glossary:

Clean – Follow the cleaning instructions to remove all grease grime and grit from the surface.
Check – Quick check to ensure level or tightness on tension is correct.
Inspect – Do a visual and physical inspection for damage, cracks and wear.
Adjust – Make regular adjustments as required
Re-assemble – Take the component apart, clean and re-assemble.
Replace – Remove old part and replace with a new part.

* Example only. Consult your dealer for a detailed maintenance program.

Engine Log

Date: ________________ Engine Number: ____________________

Engine: ______________________ Engine Builder: ____________________

Carburetor: ____

Main Jet: ____________ Pilot: _____________ Needle: _________________

Air Screw: ___________ Tube: ____________ Air Filter: ________________

Ignition Number: _______________ Ignition Curve: _____________________

Pipe: ______________________ Silencer: __________________________

Pre-mix Ratio: _______________

Fuel: ______________________ Oil: _____________________________

Water Temp.: _________ Head Temp.: __________ Max. RPM: ___________

Session: _____________ Event: _______________ Laps: _______________

Notes:

____

____

____

____

Examples of carburetor setting depending on symptom

symptom	setting	checking
At full throttle Stall at high speeds *Hard Breathing Shearing noise Whitish spark plug Lean mixture	Increase main jet calibration no. (Gradually)	Discoloration of spark plug If tan color, it is in good condition If cannot be corrected: Clogged float valve seat Clogged fuel hose Clogged fuel cock
At full throttle Speed pick-up stops Slow speed pick-up Slow response Sooty spark plug Rich mixture	Decrease main jet calibration no. (Gradually) *In case of racing slight enrichment of mixture reduces engine trouble.	Discoloration of spark plug If tan color, it is in good condition If cannot be corrected: Clogged air filter Fuel overflow from carburetor
Lean mixture	Use needle jet wiith a smaller diameter, or NBLF. Lower jet needle clip position.	
Rich mixture	Use needle jet with a larger diameter, or NBKG. Raise jet needle clip position.	
1/4 ~ 3/4 throttle *Hard breathing Lack of speed	Use jet needle with a smaller diameter, or NBLF. Lower jet needle clip position.	
1/4 ~ 1/2 throttle Slow speed pick-up White smoke	Use needle jet with a larger diameter, or NBKG. Raise jet needle clip position.	The clip position is the jet needle groove on which the clip is installed. The positions are numbered from the top.
Closed to 1/4 throttle *Hard breathing Speed down Poor acceleration White smoke	Use jet needle with a smaller diameter. Turn out pilot air screw. Turn in pilot screw.	
Unstable at low speeds Pinging noise	Lower jet needle clip position. (1 groove down) Turn in pilot screw.	
Poor response at extremely low speed	Reduce pilot jet cailbration no. Turn out pilot air screw. If no effect, reverse the above procedures.	Dragging brake Overrflow from carburetor.
Poor response in the low to intermediate speeds	Raise jet needle clip position. If this has no effect, lower the jet need clip position.	Check air filter for fouling.
Poor response when throttle is opened quickly	Check overall settings. Use main jet with a lower calibration no. Raise jet needle clip position. Use jet needle with a larger diamter. If these have no effect, use a main jet with a higher calibration no. and lower the jet needle clip position.	Check air filter for fouling.
Poor engine operation	Turn in pilot air screw. Adjust the throttle stop screw.	Check throttle valve operation.

* In case of hard breathnig, check the carburetor breather hoses for clogging.

Gear Ratio Matrix

Front Sprocket	Rear Gear 21	22	23	24	25	26	27	28	29	30
13	1.6154	1.6923	1.7692	1.8462	1.9231	2.0000	2.0769	2.1538	2.2308	2.3077
14	1.5000	1.5714	1.6429	1.7143	1.7857	1.8571	1.9286	2.0000	2.0714	2.1429
15	1.4000	1.4667	1.5333	1.6000	1.6667	1.7333	1.8000	1.8667	1.9333	2.0000
16	1.3125	1.3750	1.4375	1.5000	1.5625	1.6250	1.6875	1.7500	1.8125	1.8750
17	1.2353	1.2941	1.3529	1.4118	1.4706	1.5294	1.5882	1.6471	1.7059	1.7647
18	1.1667	1.2222	1.2778	1.3333	1.3889	1.4444	1.5000	1.5556	1.6111	1.6667
19	1.1053	1.1579	1.2105	1.2632	1.3158	1.3684	1.4211	1.4737	1.5263	1.5789
20	1.0500	1.1000	1.1500	1.2000	1.2500	1.3000	1.3500	1.4000	1.4500	1.5000

Gear Ratio By Front Gear

Front	Rear	Ratio	Front	Rear	Ratio	Front	Rear	Ratio	Front	Rear	Ratio
	21	1.615		21	1.400		21	1.235		21	1.105
	22	1.692		22	1.467		22	1.294		22	1.158
	23	1.769		23	1.533		23	1.353		23	1.211
	24	1.846		24	1.600		24	1.412		24	1.263
13	25	1.923	15	25	1.667	17	25	1.471	19	25	1.316
	26	2.000		26	1.733		26	1.529		26	1.368
	27	2.077		27	1.800		27	1.588		27	1.421
	28	2.154		28	1.867		28	1.647		28	1.474
	29	2.231		29	1.933		29	1.706		29	1.526
	30	2.308		30	2.000		30	1.765		30	1.579
	21	1.500		21	1.313		21	1.167		21	1.050
	22	1.571		22	1.375		22	1.222		22	1.100
	23	1.643		23	1.438		23	1.278		23	1.150
	24	1.714		24	1.500		24	1.333		24	1.200
14	25	1.786	16	25	1.563	18	25	1.389	20	25	1.250
	26	1.857		26	1.625		26	1.444		26	1.300
	27	1.929		27	1.688		27	1.500		27	1.350
	28	2.000		28	1.750		28	1.556		28	1.400
	29	2.071		29	1.813		29	1.611		29	1.450
	30	2.143		30	1.875		30	1.667		30	1.500

Gear Chart By Ratio

Ratio	Front	Rear	Ratio	Front	Rear	Ratio	Front	Rear
1.050	20	21	1.438	16	23	1.692	13	22
1.100	20	22	1.444	18	26	1.706	17	29
1.105	19	21	1.450	20	29	1.714	14	24
1.150	20	23	1.467	15	22	1.733	15	26
1.158	19	22	1.471	17	25	1.750	16	28
1.167	18	21	1.474	19	28	1.765	17	30
1.200	20	24	1.500	14	21	1.769	13	23
1.211	19	23	1.500	16	24	1.786	14	25
1.222	18	22	1.500	18	27	1.800	15	27
1.235	17	21	1.500	20	30	1.813	16	29
1.250	20	25	1.526	19	29	1.846	13	24
1.263	19	24	1.529	17	26	1.857	14	26
1.278	18	23	1.533	15	23	1.867	15	28
1.294	17	22	1.556	18	28	1.875	16	30
1.300	20	26	1.563	16	25	1.923	13	25
1.313	16	21	1.571	14	22	1.929	14	27
1.316	19	25	1.579	19	30	1.933	15	29
1.333	18	24	1.588	17	27	2.000	13	26
1.350	20	27	1.600	15	24	2.000	14	28
1.353	17	23	1.611	18	29	2.000	15	30
1.368	19	26	1.615	13	21	2.071	14	29
1.375	16	22	1.625	16	26	2.077	13	27
1.389	18	25	1.643	14	23	2.143	14	30
1.400	15	21	1.647	17	28	2.154	13	28
1.400	20	28	1.667	15	25	2.231	13	29
1.412	17	24	1.667	18	30	2.308	13	30
1.421	19	27	1.688	16	27			

Gear Ratio By Speed

RPM: 12,500 Tire Size: 11.00 PI=3.1416 Drive Ratio: 0.300

Front	Rear	Ratio A	Ratio B	2.307 1st	1.866 2nd	1.529 3rd	1.286 4th	1.130 5th	1.000 6th
19	21	1.105	0.905	48.13	59.50	72.62	86.34	98.26	111.03
19	22	1.158	0.864	45.94	56.80	69.32	82.41	93.79	105.98
18	21	1.167	0.857	45.59	56.37	68.79	81.79	93.09	105.19
19	23	1.211	0.826	43.94	54.33	66.30	78.83	89.71	101.38
18	22	1.222	0.818	43.52	53.81	65.67	78.08	88.86	100.41
17	21	1.235	0.810	43.06	53.24	64.97	77.25	87.91	99.34
19	24	1.263	0.792	42.11	52.06	63.54	75.55	85.98	97.15
18	23	1.278	0.783	41.63	51.47	62.81	74.68	84.99	96.04
17	22	1.294	0.773	41.10	50.82	62.02	73.74	83.92	94.83
16	21	1.313	0.762	40.53	50.11	61.15	72.71	82.74	93.50
19	25	1.316	0.760	40.43	49.98	61.00	72.52	82.54	93.27
18	24	1.333	0.750	39.90	49.32	60.20	71.57	81.45	92.04
17	23	1.353	0.739	39.32	48.61	59.32	70.53	80.27	90.71
19	26	1.368	0.731	38.87	48.06	58.65	69.73	79.36	89.68
16	22	1.375	0.727	38.69	47.83	58.37	69.40	78.98	89.25
18	25	1.389	0.720	38.30	47.35	57.79	68.71	78.19	88.36
15	21	1.400	0.714	38.00	46.98	57.33	68.16	77.57	87.66
17	24	1.412	0.708	37.68	46.58	56.85	67.59	76.93	86.93
19	27	1.421	0.704	37.43	46.28	56.48	67.15	76.42	86.36
16	23	1.438	0.696	37.00	45.75	55.83	66.38	75.55	85.37
18	26	1.444	0.692	36.83	45.53	55.57	66.06	75.19	84.96
15	22	1.467	0.682	36.27	44.84	54.72	65.06	74.05	83.67
17	25	1.471	0.680	36.17	44.72	54.58	64.89	73.85	83.45
19	28	1.474	0.679	36.10	44.63	54.46	64.75	73.69	83.27
14	21	1.500	0.667	35.46	43.84	53.51	63.62	72.40	81.81
16	24	1.500	0.667	35.46	43.84	53.51	63.62	72.40	81.81
18	27	1.500	0.667	35.46	43.84	53.51	63.62	72.40	81.81
19	29	1.526	0.655	34.85	43.09	52.58	62.52	71.15	80.40
17	26	1.529	0.654	34.78	43.00	52.48	62.39	71.01	80.24
15	23	1.533	0.652	34.69	42.89	52.34	62.23	70.83	80.03
18	28	1.556	0.643	34.20	42.28	51.60	61.35	69.81	78.89
16	25	1.563	0.640	34.04	42.09	51.37	61.07	69.50	78.54
14	22	1.571	0.636	33.85	41.85	51.08	60.73	69.11	78.09
17	27	1.588	0.630	33.49	41.41	50.53	60.08	68.38	77.27
15	24	1.600	0.625	33.25	41.10	50.16	59.64	67.88	76.70
18	29	1.611	0.621	33.02	40.82	49.82	59.23	67.41	76.17
16	26	1.625	0.615	32.73	40.47	49.39	58.72	66.83	75.52
14	23	1.643	0.609	32.38	40.03	48.85	58.09	66.10	74.70
17	28	1.647	0.607	32.30	39.93	48.73	57.94	65.94	74.51
15	25	1.667	0.600	31.92	39.46	48.16	57.26	65.16	73.63
16	27	1.688	0.593	31.52	38.97	47.56	56.55	64.36	72.72
17	29	1.706	0.586	31.18	38.55	47.05	55.94	63.66	71.94
14	24	1.714	0.583	31.03	38.36	46.82	55.67	63.35	71.59
15	26	1.733	0.577	30.69	37.94	46.30	55.05	62.65	70.80
16	28	1.750	0.571	30.40	37.58	45.86	54.53	62.06	70.13
14	25	1.786	0.560	29.79	36.83	44.95	53.44	60.82	68.72
15	27	1.800	0.556	29.55	36.54	44.59	53.01	60.33	68.18
16	29	1.813	0.552	29.35	36.28	44.28	52.65	59.92	67.71
14	26	1.857	0.538	28.64	35.41	43.22	51.38	58.48	66.08
15	28	1.867	0.536	28.50	35.23	43.00	51.12	58.18	65.74
14	27	1.929	0.519	27.58	34.10	41.62	49.48	56.31	63.63
15	29	1.933	0.517	27.51	34.02	41.51	49.36	56.17	63.48
14	28	2.000	0.500	26.60	32.88	40.13	47.71	54.30	61.36
14	29	2.071	0.483	25.68	31.75	38.75	46.07	52.43	59.24

US Measurement Gas to Oil Mixing Matrix

US Gal	US Ounces							
	20:1	21:1	22:1	23:1	24:1	25:1	26:1	27:1
1.00	6.400	6.095	5.818	5.565	5.333	5.120	4.923	4.741
1.50	9.600	9.143	8.727	8.348	8.000	7.680	7.385	7.111
2.00	12.800	12.190	11.636	11.130	10.667	10.240	9.846	9.481
2.50	16.000	15.238	14.545	13.913	13.333	12.800	12.308	11.852
3.00	19.200	18.286	17.455	16.696	16.000	15.360	14.769	14.222
3.50	22.400	21.333	20.364	19.478	18.667	17.920	17.231	16.593
4.00	25.600	24.381	23.273	22.261	21.333	20.480	19.692	18.963
4.50	28.800	27.429	26.182	25.043	24.000	23.040	22.154	21.333
5.00	32.000	30.476	29.091	27.826	26.667	25.600	24.615	23.704
5.50	35.200	33.524	32.000	30.609	29.333	28.160	27.077	26.074
6.00	38.400	36.571	34.909	33.391	32.000	30.720	29.538	28.444
6.50	41.600	39.619	37.818	36.174	34.667	33.280	32.000	30.815
7.00	44.800	42.667	40.727	38.957	37.333	35.840	34.462	33.185
7.50	48.000	45.714	43.636	41.739	40.000	38.400	36.923	35.556
8.00	51.200	48.762	46.545	44.522	42.667	40.960	39.385	37.926
8.50	54.400	51.810	49.455	47.304	45.333	43.520	41.846	40.296
9.00	57.600	54.857	52.364	50.087	48.000	46.080	44.308	42.667
9.50	60.800	57.905	55.273	52.870	50.667	48.640	46.769	45.037
10.00	64.000	60.952	58.182	55.652	53.333	51.200	49.231	47.407

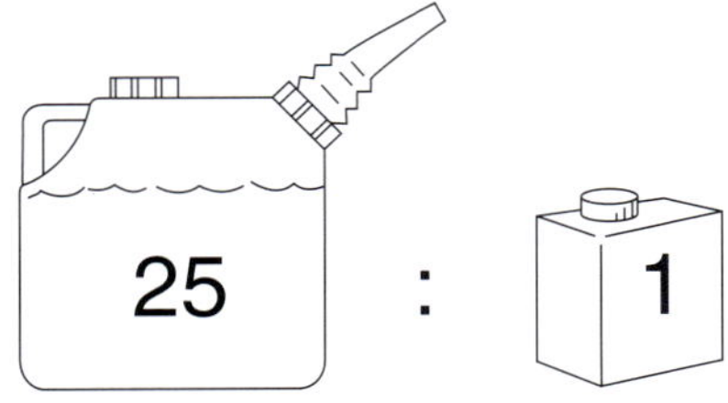

warning

Race gasoline is highly flammable. Never refuel in the vicinity of an open flame, or while smoking. Keep all fuels out of the reach of children.

GASOLINE CAN CAUSE INJURY.

Imperial Measurement Gas to Oil Mixing Matrix

Imp. Gal	Imperial Ounces 20:1	21:1	22:1	23:1	24:1	25:1	26:1	27:1
1.00	8.000	7.619	7.273	6.957	6.667	6.400	6.154	5.926
1.50	12.000	11.429	10.909	10.435	10.000	9.600	9.231	8.889
2.00	16.000	15.238	14.545	13.913	13.333	12.800	12.308	11.85
2.50	20.000	19.048	18.182	17.391	16.667	16.000	15.385	14.815
3.00	24.000	22.857	21.818	20.870	20.000	19.200	18.462	17.778
3.50	28.000	26.667	25.455	24.348	23.333	22.400	21.538	20.741
4.00	32.000	30.476	29.091	27.826	26.667	25.600	24.615	23.704
4.50	36.000	34.286	32.727	31.304	30.000	28.800	27.692	26.667
5.00	40.000	38.095	36.364	34.783	33.333	32.000	30.769	29.630
5.50	44.000	41.905	40.000	38.261	36.667	35.200	33.846	32.593
6.00	48.000	45.714	43.636	41.739	40.000	38.400	36.923	35.556
6.50	52.000	49.524	47.273	45.217	43.333	41.600	40.000	38.519
7.00	56.000	53.333	50.909	48.696	46.667	44.800	43.077	41.481
7.50	60.000	57.143	54.545	52.174	50.000	48.000	46.154	44.444
8.00	64.000	60.952	58.182	55.652	53.333	51.200	49.231	47.407
8.50	68.000	64.762	61.818	59.130	56.667	54.400	52.308	50.370
9.00	72.000	68.571	65.455	62.609	60.000	57.600	55.385	53.333
9.50	76.000	72.381	69.091	66.087	63.333	60.800	58.462	56.296
10.00	80.000	76.190	72.727	69.565	66.667	64.000	61.538	59.259

:

warning

Race gasoline is highly flammable. Never refuel in the vicinity of an open flame, or while smoking. Keep all fuels out of the reach of children.

GASOLINE CAN CAUSE INJURY.

Scaling Chart

Date: ____________ Kart: ____________ Driver: ____________

Location: ____________ Engine: ____________ Class Weight: ____________

Tire: ____________ Wheel: ____________ Other: ____________

Left	Front	Right
______ %	______ %	______ %
______ lbs/kg	______ lbs/kg	______ lbs/kg
Caster: ______		Caster: ______
Toe: ______	______ Front Track	Toe: ______
Run Out: ______		Run Out: ______
PSI: ______		PSI: ______

Draw in placement of lead.

Left	Rear	Right
Run Out: ______		Run Out: ______
PSI: ______		PSI: ______
______ %	______ Rear Track	______ %
______ lbs/kg	______ lbs/kg	______ lbs/kg
	______ %	
	Rear	

______ %		______ %
______ lbs/kg	______	______ lbs/kg
Total	Total	Total

Notes:

____

____

____

____

Baseline Set-up

Date: ____________ Kart: ____________ Driver: ____________

Location: ____________ Engine: ____________ Class Weight: ____________

Tire: ____________ Wheel: ____________ Other: ____________

Front Track ____________

Spindle: ________ Spindle: ________

Camber: ________ Camber: ________

Caster: ________ Caster: ________

Toe: ________ Toe: ________

Run Out: ________ Run Out: ________

PSI: ________ PSI: ________

Run Out: ________ Run Out: ________

PSI: ________ PSI: ________

Offset: ________ Offset: ________

Height: ________ Height: ________

Rear Track ____________

Axel ____________

Hubs: ____________ Torsion Bar: ____________ 4th Rail: ____________

Front Gear: ____________ Rear Gear: ____________ Ratio: ____________

Notes:

Race Day Set-up

Date: ____________ Track: ______________ Event: ____________________

Class: ____________ Kart: ______________ Engine: ____________________

Session: ________________________________

Hot: ____ Cold: ____ Front Track ____ Cold: ____ Hot: ____

Rear Track ____

Notes: ____________

Gear: ______ x ______

Jetting: ______ / ______

Ignition: ____________

Curve: ____________

Plug Reading: ____________

Session: ________________________________

Hot: ____ Cold: ____ Front Track ____ Cold: ____ Hot: ____

Rear Track ____

Notes: ____________

Gear: ______ x ______

Jetting: ______ / ______

Ignition: ____________

Curve: ____________

Plug Reading: ____________

Session: ________________________________

Hot: ____ Cold: ____ Front Track ____ Cold: ____ Hot: ____

Rear Track ____

Notes: ____________

Gear: ______ x ______

Jetting: ______ / ______

Ignition: ____________

Curve: ____________

Plug Reading: ____________

Pre-Race Tuning Checklist

Track: ________________ Date: ________________ By: ________________

Time	Temp.	Humidity	Barometer	Oxygen	Ignition	Jet Size

General Torque Specifications

This chart specifies torque for standard fasteners with standard I.S.O. pitch threads. To avoid warpage, tighten multi-fastener assemblies in a crisscross fashion, in progressive stages, until full torque is reached. Unless otherwise specified, torque specifications call for clean, dry threads. Components should be at room temperature.

A (Nut)	B (Bolt)	TORQUE SPECIFICATION		
		Nm	m•kg	ft•lb
10mm	6mm	6	0.6	4.3
12mm	8mm	15	1.5	11
14mm	10mm	30	3.0	22
17mm	12mm	55	5.5	40
19mm	14mm	85	8.5	61
22mm	16mm	130	13	94

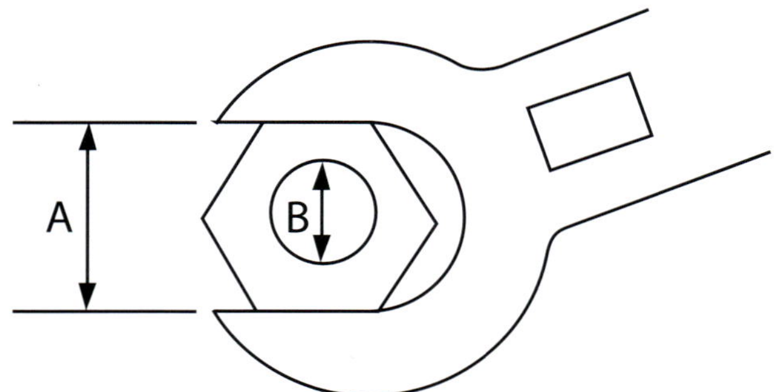

Reprinted courtesy of wewantmetric.com.
Not actual size. For reference purposes only. Consult your dealer for hardware specifications.

Metric Nut and Bolt Guide

	Hex Head	Flat Head	Socket Cap	Nut / Washer
M6 Partial Threading: Fo bolts 25mm to 125mm is 18mm Drill size: M6 / 15/64 Thread size: 1.0	length, 18mm	length	length	10 12 6.4
Wrench Size:	M10	T4	T5	M10
M8 Partial Threading: For bolts 35mm to 125mm is 22mm Drill size: M8 / 5/16 Thread size: 1.25	length, 22mm	length	length	16 16 8.4
Wrench Size:	M13	T5	T6	M13
M10 Partial Threading: For bolts 40mm to 125mm is 26mm Drill size: M10 / 13/32 Thread size: 1.5	length, 26mm	length	length	20 20 10.5
Wrench Size:	M16	T6	T8	M16

Reprinted courtesy of wewantmetric.com.
Not actual size. For reference purposes only. Consult your dealer for hardware specifications.

Mathematical Formulas

LENGTH

1 meter = 3.28 feet

1 foot = 0.30 m

1 millimeter = 0.0393 inch

Converting millimeters to inches use the formula: millimeters ÷ 25.4 = inches

Converting inches to millimeters use the formula: inches x 25.4 = millimeters

WEIGHT

1 gram = 0.0353 US oz

1 kilogram = 2.2046 lbs

TEMPERATURE

Celsius to Fahrenheit (°C x 1.8) + 32 = °F

Fahrenheit to Celsius [(°F - 32) x 5] ÷ 9 = °C

DISTANCE

For distance and speed, one mile equals 1.609 kilometers and one kilometer equals .6214 mile.

To convert kilometers to miles, use the formula: Kilometers ÷ 1.609 = miles

To convert miles to kilometers, use the formula: Miles x 1.609 = kilometers

LIQUID CAPACITY

One U.S. gallon = 3.7854 liters

One liter = .264 U.S. gallon

One U.S. quart equals .946 liter (946 cc)

The formula for converting liters to U.S. gallons is: Liters ÷ 3.7854 = U.S. gallons

Convert U.S. gallons to liters with the formula: U.S. gallons x 3.785 = liters

Liters are converted to U.S. quarts with the formula: Liters ÷ .946 = U.S. quarts

U.S. quarts are converted to liters with the formula: U.S. quarts x .946 = liters

Fraction to Decimal Conversion Chart

1/64 = .015625	17/64 = .265625	33/64 = .515625	49/64 = .765625
1/32 = .03125	9/32 = .28125	17/32 = .53125	25/32 = .78125
3/64 = .046875	19/64 = .296875	35/64 = .546875	51/64 = .796875
1/16 = .0625	**5/16 = .3125**	**9/16 = .5625**	**13/16 = .8125**
5/64 = .078125	21/64 = .328125	37/64 = .578125	53/64 = .828125
3/32 = .09375	11/32 = .34375	19/32 = .59375	27/32 = .84375
7/64 = .109375	23/64 = .359375	39/64 = .609375	55/64 = .859375
1/8 = .125	**3/8 = .375**	**5/8 = .625**	**7/8 = .875**
9/64 = .140625	25/64 = .390625	41/64 = .640625	57/64 = .890625
5/32 = .15625	13/32 = .40625	21/32 = .65625	29/32 = .90625
11/64 = .171875	27/64 = .421875	43/64 = .671875	59/64 = .921875
3/16 = .1875	**7/16 = .4375**	**11/16 = .6875**	**15/16 = .9375**
13/64 = .203125	29/64 = .453125	45/64 = .703125	61/64 = .953125
7/32 = .21875	15/32 = .46875	23/32 = .71875	31/32 = .96875
15/64 = .234375	31/64 = .484375	47/64 = .734375	63/64 = .984375
1/4 = .25	**1/2 = .5**	**3/4 = .75**	**1 = 1**

Expense Worksheet

Event: ________________ To: ________________ From: ________________

Date	Gas	Meals	Fees	Supplies	Parts	Total
Total:						

Notes:

Check out our nuts...
www.wewantmetric.com
...and bolts!

BEACON ON TRACK

RLV

THRASHER

tm RACING

Douglas Wheel